Daddy Why Don't You Love Me?

A Father's Blessing to a Daughter

Healing the Wounds of the Absent and Abusive Father

Papa Ray Hurst

i

Disclaimer

The content of this book is for informational purposes only and is not intended to diagnose, treat, cure, or prevent depression or anxiety.

Please consult with a professional physician, counselor, or therapist if you feel depressed, suicidal, or have the desire to harm yourself in any way.

The publisher and author (Papa Ray Hurst, Team Jesus Ministries, and ILAP Coaching) make no guarantees concerning the level of success you may experience by following the advice and strategies in this book. You accept that results will differ for each individual.

The testimonies and examples provided in this book show exceptional results. These may not apply to the average reader and are not intended to represent or guarantee that you will achieve the same or similar results.

The apology letters written in this book in no way implicate the author, Ray Hurst, or his family as responsible for any past event in your life or the lives of the individuals in this book. The author, Ray Hurst, any and all editors, publishers, printers, resellers, or any party involved with the distribution of this book (including all businesses owned in whole or in part by Ray Hurst, Willa Hurst, or the Hurst family – including and not limited to Team Jesus Ministries and ILAP Coaching) cannot be held responsible for damages or mental, financial, physical, or emotional harm for anything they did not have a part in (that was caused in whole or in part by another party not involving them).

Acknowledgments

First and foremost, thank you to my awesome wife, **Willa Hurst**, for helping to make my dreams possible. I would never have been able to do this without you. You're a rock star in my life, and I love you!

Marjorie Solon: You're the inspiration for this book. It's been an honor and a pleasure to be a mentor in your life. I praise God that He has allowed me to have part in helping you to become the amazing woman of God you are! I love you forever!

Maria Assunção: I know I would never have been able to touch the hearts and minds of the thousands of people in Brazil if you hadn't been there. Thank you for pouring out your heart and love to so many. Love you Mom!

Brenda Joy Woggon: Thank you for putting up with me where this all started – my first mission trip to Brazil! You truly are an amazing, patient, and kindhearted woman of God. I'll never forget DQ: "Die quietly." I'm so blessed because of you; thank you again. I love you so much!

Pr. Marcelo Mendonça Ramos: Thank you for your friendship, encouragement, and for helping me along the way!

Pr. José Carlos Baptista: Thank you for all you have done to help over the years, you have been a huge part in helping to make all this happen. I love you my brother!

Pr. Elizabete Salgado: Thank you for all you have done as well. You truly are the example of a woman after Gods own heart. You will be in my heart forever. I love you!

Randy Clark: Thank you for building Global Awakening. It's become a platform for so many ministries to start. I pray that many more will reap a harvest from what you have sown.

Jack Frost: I've learned a lot from Jack – the founder of Shiloh Place Ministry – over the years. I'm very thankful for all the work he has done and for being a forerunner in the ministry of fathering.

John Sandford: I want to give John – the founder of Elijah House – special recognition. I first heard about standing in the place of a father by listening to one of his teachings. If I hadn't heard that, I'm not sure this work would have ever begun in 2004.

Thank you to our donors for believing in me and helping to get these books on the market.

Gold Sponsors

Elvin Hurst

Silver Sponsors

Dr. Clair Zimmerman

Table of Contents

References 148

Introduction

This book is all about you, girl.

This book was written to bless every girl or woman who has ever felt forsaken or abandoned by their earthly father. I want you to know and believe you're worthy. This blessing is for you – no matter your background or beliefs. If you've ever felt alone or rejected by your father – or a father figure – I want to stand in that place and bless you. You're worthy to be blessed and loved!

No matter what lifestyle you lead, what religion you practice, or if you don't follow any faith, I want you to know **you are loved**. I want to help restore love, hope, and faith into your life and lift you up to where you belong. This book's purpose is to help you see that you're not abandoned or forsaken; you truly are loved with a pure and true love. I encourage you to be all you were born to be!

You can jump over the moon and touch the stars.

I want to be a father to the fatherless – touching the brokenhearted and leaving the fingerprints of Jesus on each heart. I call up the purpose borne in each and every woman and girl! I call to the depth of the child inside you, shouting:

> *"Stand up! Rise up – for your day has come. You are worthy. Come and fulfill your destiny; don't let life pass you by."*

I pray that every woman and girl reading this book will receive the Father's Blessing in her heart. It's my hope that everyone who receives the Father's Blessing will have their broken heart healed and restored. I share the heart of an earthly father so that you may become better equipped for life's journey. I want you – and all women – to be blessed and strengthened for the journey that lies ahead. By showing you a father's love, I want to break down the barriers that stop you from becoming all you were created to be. By showing you the love and respect you deserve, I want to empower women and girls like you to become the awesome creations that God intended you to be.

I'm so excited to be sharing this blessing with you. I know you'll be able to learn and grow. You are amazing, and I'm looking forward to seeing you become all that you were made to be!

Please read each chapter with care and as many times as needed. Throughout each chapter, I'll include thought-provoking questions. I suggest you keep a notebook to answer them. This is a way of making each chapter more personal to you and your life.

From Brokenness to Healing Hearts and Minds

I've had my share of battles along the way, and I'm sure that's the reason I'm a personal transformation coach today. I want to be for the world what the world wasn't for me when I needed them the most. I now know that others couldn't give me what they didn't have. Now I want to give what I have – so others can be more and do more! I've known the sting and empty feeling of rejection almost all my life. If I can do it, I know you can too!

I grew up in a single-parent home; my father left my mother and two older brothers when I was four years old. I knew the pain of longing to be loved by a father. I never knew how to properly deal with the love deficit that was in my heart. As a result, I carried a lot of the struggles from my childhood into adulthood. At the time,

I didn't understand that it was a love deficit. I thought everyone else had a problem and that my actions weren't my fault. I thought that if others did everything the way I wanted them to, the whole world would be a better place. I now realize that the larger part of my life's struggles could have been avoided if I understood some of this back then!

Now I see that more people are broken than healthy – and most are just as broken (or even more so) than I was. They need to be loved – the same as I did. Some people are just better at hiding their emptiness than others. I, however, was never good at hiding my pain or emptiness.

I've always lived life out loud. I was always very quick to tell people what I thought. It didn't matter how right I was – people got offended when I told them they were wrong. At the time, I justified my actions by thinking that *someone* had to tell them the truth. There was only one problem with that: They didn't want to be corrected any more than I did. We often were just two empty, broken people trying to fix each other!

The world is full of empty and broken people. Unless you live in a cave, it'll be hard to avoid them. The good news is that I've learned a lot about dealing with these people. Throughout this book, I'll share some of the things I've learned over the years – things that have helped me reshape my life and deal with pain and misunderstandings. I want to speak into your life and encourage you as a loving, caring father – so that you don't stumble over the same pebbles that I did.

I write this to you in hopes that you'll be able to understand what happened in your past and why. It's important not to bury the pain of the past – it never truly goes away. The only way you can heal from what happened is to change the meaning you give to it! I hope you'll find the strength to face the past and write the truth of who you are – no matter what happened. Your past does not have to be your future; you have the power to change your future – by changing the meaning you give to your past!

Stop and Reflect

- How have you tried to fill the feelings of emptiness or rejection due to your father's absence?

- How do you see yourself after growing up with an absent or abusive father?

- In what ways have feelings of brokenness or emptiness affected your life?

The First Mission Trip

My first mission trip to Brazil was in 2004. It didn't take me long to adopt an amazing and wonderful lady, Brenda Woggan, as my mother. This broken, empty little boy needed someone to steer him back gently and lovingly to reality. Momma Brenda was just the kind and gentle – yet firm – voice of reason to do just that. When I got on the bus after meetings and complained to her – in all her wisdom and love – she would say, "DQ, my son. DQ."

I asked, "What do you mean by DQ?" She replied with a smile, "Die quietly." It's true – I never knew how to die quietly. Thank you, Momma Brenda, for your great words of wisdom! I love you! We need more people like you – people who can stand as a gentle and firm voice of reason!

This mission trip was hosted by Global Awakening. Over the years, I had gotten to know more about their work. When I found out about their planned trip to Brazil, something clicked – I knew I needed to go!

On Global Awakenings mission trips the main focus is praying for supernatural physical healing and spiritual deliverance. I attended the mandatory training class in Mechanicsburg, Pennsylvania, before I went on the trip. The training class was a fantastic time of learning and growing in my understanding and faith. The mission trip was one of the most pivotal events in my life! I was changed forever.

This two-week mission trip took us to two different cities in Brazil. For the first part of the trip, we were in a small coastal city in the northeast part of the country. We made one very special stop in route to Pato Branco. We stopped at Iguazu Falls, which borders Argentina near Paraguay. Iguazu Falls is one of the largest falls in the world.

Pato Branco translated into English means "white duck." It's a small city of about 80,000 people in the southwestern part of the Brazilian state of Paraná. This little city was the starting point for one of the most fantastic turning points in my life!

Like so many other things in life, my ministry started as one simple act of love. It grew unexpectedly into a powerful, life-changing movement around the world. Never forget; it all begins with the first step. If you aren't willing to take the first step, you'll never be great at anything. As I like to say:

> *"Give without expectation, and it will be given back to you in the same heart you gave. If you want more, give more!"*

We stayed in Pato Branco for five days. Every day, we took the tour bus to a church on the edge of town. I would estimate that the church could seat a few hundred people. In the afternoons, we held classes and trainings for people who wanted to learn more about healing and deliverance. When evening came, we held open meetings for anyone who wanted to hear the message and receive prayer. Every night, we had someone teach more about healing and deliverance. After the message, our team spread out around the church as people came for prayer. Most of us didn't speak Portuguese, the primary language in Brazil, so we always had a translator with us.

On the second or third day in Pato Branco, a young lady in her early twenties came to me for prayer. I don't remember why she initially asked for prayer. All I can remember is that the Holy Spirit told me to stand in place of her earthly father and bless her as a daughter. I had never done anything like this before – this wasn't part of the training we received before the trip. I was in uncharted territory and going totally off-the-cuff. At the time, I vaguely remembered that John Sandford of Elijah House Ministries said something about standing in place as a father for someone in one of his classes about four or five years before.

I was a little unsure about it at first but decided that the most she could do was say no. I asked her if I could stand in the place of her father and bless her – and she agreed. Neither of us could ever have guessed what would happen next!

First, I asked her forgiveness for the wrongs committed by her father. I asked her to forgive me for not loving her the way a father should have loved his daughter. I asked her to forgive me for all the harsh words I had spoken to her. I told her that it wasn't her fault – she didn't do anything to deserve any of it! I told her that it was my fault that I didn't show her the love I should have – not hers.

A moment of doubt flashed through my mind as she doubled over in pain – grasping her stomach and weeping profusely. I never expected this kind of reaction. As I held her other hand, I was overwhelmed with emotions – fear and doubt started rushing through my mind! I thought that – like usual – I would pray for people, and they would be healed, happy, and dance with joy.

At this moment, that wasn't happening. Something deep inside of me knew that she needed to get more of this out.

When you aren't willing to feel pain, you'll push it back down – only for it to come back up another time. The pain we push down will come out in other ways – in other places. So I pressed on. I told her I was so sorry that I wasn't there to hold her as a little girl. Wow, that opened a new floodgate of pain! She wept more. At the time, I thought I was grasping at straws – hoping to say something to ease the pain. Now I know that the Holy Spirit was guiding me and telling me what to say. The more I said, the more she wept!

I told her how wrong I was for not being there and that I was the one that lost out. I asked her to forgive me for what I did wrong – because forgiveness is the key to healing. Without forgiveness, there can't be healing.

After a few moments of coming to grips with everything I said – things her father never shared – she was able to say, "I forgive you." I wanted to make sure she hadn't forgiven the person sharing the blessing – but rather, her father… And she had. She forgave him for everything.

I went on to bless her, affirm her as a daughter, and tell her how important she was. I told her that she was loved and that she was wanted. What a transformation! Tears of pain turned to tears of joy! She was able to tear down the lies of feeling rejected and abandoned. She heard the truth of who she truly was – not the lies she had built in her mind. All the years without hearing loving and affectionate words of care and compassion from her father had taken their toll.

Sometimes what we don't hear can cause as much damage as what we do hear from our parents. It's the same as neglecting to put all the blocks in the foundation of a building – but still expecting it to be secure. This simple act of love and truth spoken from my heart to hers was so powerful that it tore down years of lies in her heart and mind.

She may have never heard a blessing from her father or even knew that he loved her. It's possible she had closed her heart to him and wasn't able to receive his love – no matter how hard he tried. Either way, this was a time of powerful, life-changing healing and restoration. No matter what happened before, I know that her life was never the same because I blessed her that day.

Since that trip, my life has become a massive outpouring – a powerful life-giving flow of God's love – that has transformed countless lives.

Stop and Reflect

- Who are the "Momma Brendas" in your life – who speak the truth to you in a loving and firm way?

The Second Trip

The next two-week trip I made to Brazil in 2006 had a much different outcome. It was another exciting, life-changing trip with Global Awakening. This time, we started in Santarém – a city in the western part of Pará, Brazil. Santarém is located where the Tapajós and Amazon Rivers meet. It was so hot that I broke into a sweat just standing in the shade! I even went swimming in the Amazon River!

By this point, I had shared the Father's Blessing for two years and had refined it a lot. As a result, I no longer panicked when someone was deeply moved by what I shared. In the second half of our two-week trip, we were in Fortaleza, Brazil – a city of three million people.

Every day when I would pray for anyone the Holy Spirit would say, "It's their father. Share the blessing with them." At first I was unsure if I was really hearing correctly. After it happen every time with everyone I would simply ask, "Can I stand in the place of your father and bless you?" As I remember, only one person in five days turned down my offer, I am not sure they understood what I meant.

However, every person who received the blessing was moved and experienced healing in their heart and mind.

During one of the sessions at Igreja da Paz (meaning "church of peace"), I shared the Father's Blessing with Marjorie Solon – a young lady who impacted my life forever. She also changed the course of my ministry forever. The day I shared the Father's Blessing with her, I never imagined that she would become a huge blessing to me – changing my life forever!

After the Trips

Once I was back home, I got a message on Facebook from Marjorie – thanking me for sharing this blessing with her. Because I had prayed for so many people, I asked her to send

Marjorie is on the right, wearing the black top.

me a photo. When she sent it, there were several other people in the picture. I felt so bad, but I had to ask her who she was! I was so afraid that I would offend her. If I didn't ask, I would've never known who she was.

When I figured out who she was, I realized that I had taken a picture with her. That story could be another book! Marjorie contacted me on Facebook Messenger, and I used Google Translate to understand her.

Me and Marjorie. Yes, that's a mullet – I had taken a vow not to cut the
back of my hair. To my surprise, I went 12 years before I cut it!

It was amazing to watch Marjorie grow over the years. I was
somehow able to make a powerful impact upon her life from
thousands of miles away – and I wasn't even able to speak the
same language. Thank you, Google, for helping me to touch
people around the world from my desk chair! Over the next
four years, I mentored her and spoke into her life with the
love and guidance of a father.

Something powerful must have gotten through – as I write
this, Marjorie has finished law school and has been traveling

around the world to study. I can't take any credit for how smart she is; she's brilliant! My goal was always to lift her up and empower her to be more; I wanted my spiritual ceiling to become her floor. I wanted to give her the running start in life I didn't have.

It was around 2010 when she said, "Papa, you have to come back to Brazil." That's where I got the name Papa Ray. When Marjorie would write, she would always call me Papa. She said, "You need to return to Brazil and share that 'father thing' you do. We really need that here!" After praying and talking with my wife, I decided I would go – but only if she found me a place to stay (with someone who spoke English) and a translator to accompany me.

Later Trips

About two weeks later, Marjorie sent me a message that she'd found a place for me to stay and a person to translate for me! This would be the first of four trips I took to Brazil with my own ministry to share the Father's Blessing! I met a lot of awesome people on each one of my trips to Brazil

I couldn't have done this without this awesome lady, Maria Assunção.

She is a retired doctor, with a heart to help others and has now become a lifelong friend and a huge part of my ministry! I could never have done anything without the generous help and love she gave me. She's been central to each of my mission trips to Brazil. I'm forever indebted to her!

Each time I traveled to Brazil was a valuable learning experience. When possible, we went to drug rehabs and prisons during the day. I'm sure it would have taken a lot longer to learn and develop my teachings any other way! I've learned so much more than I ever thought I would. If you told me what I would go through and learn, I never would've believed it!

Always be open to learning. Be open to understanding new things – when you close your mind, you stop learning! I'm so glad you're reading this book; if you keep your heart open and have a desire to be more, I know you'll be blessed by what you learn!

I really want to honor Marjorie and Maria as huge inspirations in my life. I would never be anywhere near where I am now if it weren't for these two resilient women. They helped make this possible. They were critical in laying the groundwork before this book was even a dream in my mind. They helped to build a foundation for what I do. Little did they know that their efforts would touch the world! They were willing to work hard and plant the seeds that someone else would enjoy the shade from in years to come!

Stop and Reflect

- Who are the people that have impacted your life in a positive way?

- Have you been able to honor those who were there when you had nothing?

If you've never taken the time to thank the ones who were there for you, please let them know how grateful you are. Every hero needs more rocket fuel!

Changed Lives

This chapter contains a few testimonies about how this blessing has changed lives. The one I remember the most was on one of my own personal mission trips to Brazil. This was one of the most dramatic reactions I've ever seen.

We were staying at a ranch in Juazeiro do Norte – in the western part of the state of Ceará, Brazil. The lady of the house asked if she could invite her son-in-law to stop by so that I could share the Father's Blessing with him. I assured her that it wouldn't be a problem, and I would be glad to. As it turned out, he had no idea what we were doing or what his mother-in-law wanted us to talk about. I used a translator who had done this with me so often that he probably could have done it without me.

I told the son-in-law that I wanted to stand in as his father and bless him. I'm not sure what he heard, but he became furious and said, "If I see that S.O.B., I'll kill him!" He was so

24

angry that if his father had walked through the door, I think he would have strangled him with his bare hands! I was taken aback by his outburst. I wasn't sure if this was such a good idea. I decided that I would at least try to share the blessing.

I asked him if I could pray for him, and he agreed. I started out like I always did. I told him that I was sorry for not being there for him as a father and for the harsh words I spoke to him as a child. He told me that his father left his mother to raise him by herself, so I made sure to say that I was sorry for abandoning them and for causing so much hardship. I then shared the blessing – starting at conception and blessing each part of his life.

The end was the part I'll never forget. This was, once again, another reminder of how powerful and life-changing this blessing really is. As I shared the blessing with him, he sat upon the floor – his back leaning against the wall. When the interpreter was done, the young man just sat there – holding his chest with both hands and gasping for air.

I was totally overwhelmed – I was sure that this guy was having a heart attack! I kept asking my translator, "What's happening? What's going on?" Imagine trying to explain this one! Here I am in a foreign country – telling people I want to set them free of their mental prison – and this guy had a heart attack on me! My translator kept saying, "I don't know what's happening. He's not talking; he doesn't answer me when I ask him anything." It felt like a long time before he caught his breath and finally spoke. What came out of his mouth stunned me. He said, "I want to see my dad." I thanked God first that this man wasn't having a heart attack – second, that he didn't want to kill his father anymore.

He had a mindset or a belief that he grew up with; he thought his dad hated him and wanted nothing to do with him. The truth was more like this: His father was a broken little boy that never healed from his own hurts and failures.

What happened to him after he heard me speak life and love over him? He had a major mind shift. He changed how he thought about his past, and it instantly set him free. It was a powerful, life-changing choice that changed his perspective. When he changed how he saw things, he removed all the anger and hate – he was able to see in a whole new way.

I have no doubt that this also changed how he dealt with other people in his life. You can't be that angry without it affecting other relationships in a negative way. Looking back,

I'm sure his mother-in-law knew he was struggling to forgive his father, and that's why she invited him over.

In Brazil, we shared in churches five and six nights a week. It was amazing and powerful! I told everyone that I wasn't a tourist and didn't want to go sight-seeing; I simply wanted to meet people and bless them.

For the most part, I'll never see the people I with whom I shared this blessing again. We were only at a particular church once – the next night, we were somewhere else. One time, though, we went to the same church two nights in a row. The first night, I told everyone that it was important to ask your parents for forgiveness for not being a better child. We need to understand that we've done things that have hurt our parents, and we need to take responsibility for those wrongs. I told everyone to go home and ask their parents to forgive them for what they did wrong.

So many times, I never heard what happened after I left a church. This time, I got to hear another beautiful testimony of a life changed because someone stepped up and asked for forgiveness. A teenage girl shared how she and her father fought all the time – she tried everything possible to avoid him. She looked forward to the day she could move out and wouldn't have to deal with him anymore. She went home the night before and did what I asked her to do. She asked her father to forgive her for not being a better daughter.

Her father sat upright in his chair and said, "What do you mean? Why are you asking me to forgive you – when I'm the one that has been wrong?" The daughter helped him find himself again. We can only speculate what happened because we never spoke to the dad – but here's what I imagine took place: The dad was lost in his own world of hurt and pain and couldn't see how much his daughter was hurting. When she asked him for forgiveness, it opened his heart and mind in a whole new way.

If you allow it to, this can happen in the snap of a finger. Sadly enough, all too many people are just angry, bitter, and unwilling to change. I've seen situations in which a daughter asked her father to bless her, and he just laughed and mocked her. It's truly sad how some people are so broken and empty – yet have no desire to find true healing. These people don't think they're doing anything wrong. They've lived this way for so long that it's become a powerful mindset – a prison, really – that they'll carry to their grave.

The way people treat you isn't because of who you are – but because of who they are. When you see that they're broken and empty, you'll see that they can't give you what they don't have.

I could write several books about how the Father's Blessing has changed people's lives. I would love to hear how this book has changed you. If you would like, share your testimony with me. Share how this has helped you. Let me know if you would allow us to include your testimony in a revised version of this book in the future. Please understand that permitting us to use your story doesn't guarantee that we'll be able to include it in the next revision.

Please send your testimony to *info@fathersblessing.info*

My Story: From Despair to Victory

Here I'll share more about what happened when I didn't put my past into perspective – when I had not yet rewritten the meaning of the difficult events in my childhood. It still affected me well into my adulthood.

I was born into a conservative Mennonite family. (No, I wasn't raised Amish!) I was raised in the Horning Mennonite Church, known locally as the "black bumper church." Because they were a very conservative religious group, they did many things to differentiate themselves from the world. Their cars were painted all black – including the bumpers. That's how they got the nickname of the "black bumper church." Like many conservative groups, they didn't allow any outside teachings or influences. They worked very hard to discredit anything they weren't doing within their leadership. The church that I grew up in wasn't – and still isn't – led by the Holy Spirit; they relied upon their own understandings within their closed group. They didn't allow televisions, radios, and – during my childhood – cameras. They tried hard to keep themselves away from the rest of the world. This isn't necessarily a bad thing.

I didn't feel any love from them. Because I didn't fit the mold they'd designed, I felt a lot of harsh condemnation from my family and the church. I had many questions about things – to which they didn't have real answers. A lot of the time, my mother would simply say, "That's just the way we do things." So much of how I was raised was based upon the phrase, "This is just the way we've always done it." The unspoken truth was that they were afraid to change anything. When I challenged their way of thinking, they became offended and said I was just rebellious.

I didn't fit in because I wasn't willing to go with the flow. I ended up hanging around with the wrong crowd, which led me into a lot of trouble. My family didn't know what to do other than what they were taught – to condemn and criticize. As you can imagine, this just drove me further away. Because I never felt that I was good enough, I always sought the approval of others. At the same time, I knew that the church leaders didn't have it together themselves. My father left our home when I was four years old – vainly chasing his dream of wealth and power – so I also felt a lot of rejection and abandonment.

I looked to other people to bring me fulfillment, hoping they would fill my emptiness. I hoped that someone would see my worth and that I had valuable ideas. Too many times, I tried to show people the way I saw things – and too many times, they weren't ready to receive what I wanted to show them.

I see now that I was often too aggressive in my approach. I also learned that a lot of people simply don't want to change – even when they know they need to.

I received a lot of backlash from people who didn't want to hear what they had done wrong. Because they had more power than I did, I suffered. One thing that helped me more than anything was the knowledge that the world is much bigger than the small group of people you know. No matter how many people you know, it's very few in comparison to the population of the world. When the people you know don't want to hear what you have to say, stop trying to tell them. Move on – the people that know you best are some of the last people to listen or accept that you've changed.

When you're walking in a new spiritual gift, this happens even more often. Sadly, many people don't like to see others rise above what they themselves have achieved – or to see others become better in any way. When they see someone they once looked down upon rising above what they themselves are, it makes them feel foolish or stagnant. They must either change the way they think about that person or come up with a lame excuse for why that person couldn't have changed.

When My Mind Ran Away

By the time I was thirty-three years old, I had allowed some of my past to drag me down. I was in the midst of a crippling depression. It was so bad that I would sleep eight to 10 hours a night – but would still wake up mentally and emotionally exhausted. I knew what I needed to do, and I knew how to do it. The hard part was that I couldn't physically do it. I knew that my boat was sinking. All I could do was sit there with a bucket in my hand and watch the boat fill up with water. In my mind, I was on a massive cruise ship. I wondered, "Why even try to bail out the water?" In reality, I was in a rowboat – my depression had blinded me.

This was the feeling of complete and utter hopelessness. My mind had run away with thoughts of feeling utterly worthless. I even felt that God didn't hear me. I envisioned that as I reached up to God, He reached His hand down to me – and I missed His hand by a few inches every time. This only drove me deeper and deeper into despair and hopelessness. The hardest part was that as I reached out for help, no one helped me – even when they easily could have.

Imagine feeling completely broken – watching your dreams slip away – and crying out for help, only to hear "just get over it" or "go out and work." You can't just stand up and shake off what got you there in the first place – no matter who tells you to. Are you crying out for help – and all you hear is the hollow echo of your own voice, bouncing off the empty walls of the hole you fell into? Have you slipped into despair and brokenness, believing that no one cares enough to even look down in the hole – let alone help you to get out? I was there myself. I know the pain of family members who had the means to help and refused – or even mocked me – as they watched me fall down over and over.

Because I didn't see results any other way, I cried out for help and attention in some not-so-good ways. I looked to people in my church for help, but they didn't have the

34

answers. They were just as broken as I was – they were just better at hiding it. I believe that being rejected by my church family hurt as much as – if not more than – the rejection I was getting from my biological family. I had a false belief that I could be real with the people in my church. I already knew that my family wouldn't accept me for who I was.

Have you ever been rejected by a church family or religious group that you thought would be there for you? Have you ever felt the sheer, stabbing pains of rejection when the leaders that you looked up to became the ones that stepped on you? It's a harsh pain to experience. Until I found the path to freedom – by renewing my mind – I lived through this for most of my life. If the truth sets you free, then if you aren't free, you don't have the truth.

The whole purpose of this book is to help you see the truth of who you are at your core – so that you can be free! I'll give you a small glimpse of what I did to win after two major depressions – the second one almost taking my life. I want to stand in for the people who hurt you and break the stranglehold they have on your life. I want to speak this powerful blessing over you – to destroy the lies you believed because of how you were treated. There's no reason you should be held down by the chains of deception – just because someone wasn't willing to help you. You don't need to carry this burden or hold this bondage in your heart anymore. I want to help you be free.

How I Beat the Odds

One day, I shared a bit of my story with a men's group. One of them asked me a crucial question: "So how did you get over it? What did you do to get through it?" That's the question of the century. The short answer is an easy one – at the same time, it was the hardest thing I ever did.

I changed my mind. In a nutshell, that's it: I simply changed my mind in terms of how I looked at other people and myself. When I realized that how I saw my past was a large part my future, I changed my perspective on life, love, and God – on what happened in my past. I learned not to allow the rock of despair from the past to fall and crush me. I stood upon that rock and climbed higher.

Doing nothing is like being on a ship without a rudder; it goes wherever the wind blows. If you don't care where you go or what happens, it doesn't matter. If you want a different outcome, you must set a different course and let go of the past. The only way you can let go is to change the meaning of what happened.

I took every part of my life – and every person in my past – and put them into perspective; I changed the meaning I gave to what happened. I understood that they couldn't give me what they didn't have. I took every part of my life and saw it

37

in the way God did. I saw it for what it was. **The truth is: They were broken and empty; they couldn't give me what they didn't have**.

Can a person who's whole and complete – in their right mind – act the same way as those who hurt you? The answer is simply: No, they couldn't. No complete and whole person would ever mistreat another. I applied this to every part of my life – every person. I couldn't leave any part untouched. I couldn't be completely healed without looking at 100% of my past. No matter how much it hurt, I unpacked it and spoke

God's truth into it. Everything is the sum of its parts – every part is needed to complete the whole thing. The same is true with a clock. If one gear isn't synchronized, the clock won't work correctly.

If you only work to improve 90% of your life, you'll never be whole. If people don't look at every part of life, they'll never be completely free or renewed. The blood of Christ doesn't set you free from something you aren't willing to let go of – nor will it forgive those who hurt you. If you want to find real freedom, you must face the struggles in every part of your life.

Many people have never healed from how their fathers treated them as children. For some, it's because their father was never in their life at all. If you don't face this issue, it can't be healed. People often say that it's nothing and that it doesn't matter anyway. They say this because they don't want to feel the pain that's still deep in their heart. I must say it again: We won't find healing and wholeness until we're willing to face the pain. The lack of a father's love is one of the deepest wounds a person can have. Sadly, so many people go to their graves without healing from this hurt.

It's very hard to look at God as a loving and kind Father when you're unable to forgive the father you have here on Earth. You must forgive your father on Earth to have a genuine relationship with your Heavenly Father. When I thought my father abandoned me, I looked at God in Heaven as a father that would do the same. I found it hard to trust in someone that I was sure wouldn't be there when I needed them.

As a young child, my father called to tell us about the big deals he was working on. Of course, I wanted to believe that everything he said was true – I always hoped that things would change for the better. He would say things like, "I just invested $10,000 in oil wells for you boys." I was so excited that we finally wouldn't have to scrape by. We would be able to buy the things we liked – we wouldn't have to buy all the cheapest things. My mother told us, "Don't believe it – he'll never do it." At the time, it seemed as if my mother was just mad at him and didn't want us to look up to him or trust him.

My father never came through with any of his big deals. He rarely even paid child support. I have very few memories of him being there. All the stories I heard were just that: Stories that never came true. I struggled for more than 54 years until I stopped looking at God the same way I looked at my father. I stopped thinking that Father God was going to abandon me – the same way my earthly father did. I stopped thinking that Father God wouldn't follow through because He was off chasing a wild dream. When I took control of my mind, I saw that I had an entirely wrong perspective of who God – as my Heavenly Father – really was.

40

If you know the Father in Heaven and you feel that He is out of reach or that He is too busy for you, receive this earthly father's blessing to break the thoughts that you aren't worthy. Allow the blessing to break the thought patterns of rejection or abandonment. It was the power of words that caused the bondage and hurt in your heart in the first place; it's the power of words that will break it.

Are you ready to open your heart and receive the love that you may have never heard before? Are you ready to be free from the feeling that you aren't good enough? The first step is to receive this blessing into your heart and firmly hold on to the truth that you're loved and wanted. If you don't let go of the hurts and wounds of the past and move forward, God Himself can't set you free. The next step is to forgive the people that hurt you. Forgiveness doesn't make them right or make you wrong; it means that you won't hold them in debt. Forgiveness doesn't mean that you need to be around that person again. Sometimes it's wise not to be around people who only hurt you.

If you don't renew your mind, reading this blessing, reading your Bible, and praying earnestly every day won't help you. The most significant step toward freedom is to take your thoughts captive and make them submit to the truth. If you don't align your thoughts with what the Word of God says, it doesn't matter how much you pray or read the Bible – nothing will change. When you know the truth, it will set you free. If you aren't walking in freedom, there's some more truth for you to find.

Stop and Reflect

- Have you been allowing the rock of despair to fall on top of you? What impact has this weight had?

- Are you ready to set a new course in life?

- What meaning have you given to some of the events in your life? Which ones do you need to change?

- Are you ready to look at all the parts of your life that aren't working? Which parts will be the most challenging?

- Do you see God in the same way you see your earthly father?

- Are you willing to forgive the people who hurt you? Who might those people be?

How to Rewrite Your Past

It's no secret that there are a lot of hurting and broken people in the world today. Drug and alcohol abuse have become ever more of a problem. When people don't find acceptance where they should (in the home), they try to find it in something else. All too many people think more sex will fill the emptiness deep inside. Sadly, this only causes more pain and suffering – it can never bring true peace of mind.

There have been incredible advances in medicine and technology; people are living much longer. With all we have to make life easier – with all we have at our fingertips – you would think people would be happier. Just turn on the television and you'll see the next greatest thing – "It'll make life better." If you buy this new car or this new house or go on this vacation, "your life will be complete." In spite of this, more and more people with fame and fortune continue to struggle deeply.

I've heard it said more often than I can count: "Money can't buy happiness." And it's true. Happiness and peace are a state of mind; to have peace, you must identify the incorrect belief that you've allowed to settle within your mind. Real and complete joy only come from having Jesus Christ as your Savior, and happiness can only come when you put your life into perspective – when you know the truth.

Some people who have followed the faith for a long time and profess Christ as their Savior are some of the most miserable people I've ever met. They haven't dealt with the hurt and pain of their past. Jesus only unlocks the door of the prison cell; it's up to the individual to either walk out or stay in the jail of their past.

Painful memories not dealt with become the bars of your prison. You are the only one who can remove them – you're a prisoner of your own mind. The fear you have is only real inside your mind. No one else sees or feels your fear in the same way as you – it's yours alone.

This also means that you're the only one that can change the way you think. Fear isn't real outside your own mind. It's been said many times: "It's all in your head." It *is* all in your head. No one else can see, hear, or experience what *you* do. You're the only one who can change how you see things – not even God can change your mind. If God could change your mind, why didn't He do so a long time ago?

If God could change your mind, that would take away your free will. You would never be able to make a bad decision again. Wow, that would be so awesome; it would be a perfect world – no one would do anything wrong... Because everyone would be perfect! But you wouldn't be *you* anymore; you would be nothing more than a robot – doing the bidding of the master who programmed you.

Making you do God's perfect will isn't love. The act of keeping something in captivity and forcing it to do what you want – just the way you want it... How could that be real love? Letting something go and allowing it to return to you out of love for you and your actions – that's real love. This is the answer to the age-old question: "If God is a loving God, why do bad things happen to good people?" Love doesn't keep things in bondage – when love sets something free, it's free to do bad things.

I struggled with the same problem that many people do. I wanted people to love and respect me. I wanted them to tell me that I was amazing and worthy; I wanted to feel important and to be part of something bigger than myself. The problem wasn't my desire to be loved and respected; the problem was that I wanted this more than anything else – it became a driving force in my life... So much so that when people didn't respond positively, I acted out more and more to get their attention.

A lot of those things didn't help me get the right kind of attention. In my desperate desire to belong, I tried to show people that I had the answers... Well, you likely know what happens when you tell people what they don't want to hear. It became an even bigger problem when I challenged those in leadership roles. It's surprising how many leaders know what to say to make themselves look good from a distance – when you get up close, they aren't what you thought they were.

Other people didn't have love to give me. They lived in their own little prisons. They were also trapped by their "ideal" way of life that was, in fact, falling apart – because they couldn't live up to the standard of other prisoners. As I've grown in wisdom and understanding, I know that my worth isn't based upon what other people think. It doesn't matter if they love or hate me. My real value and freedom come from knowing Jesus Christ as my Lord and Savior.

Please allow me to clarify one thing; you can't go around with your fingers stuck in your ears – without listening to what others say. You must hear what other people are saying about and to you. No one is perfect; we all need insight and direction in our lives. I'm a strong supporter of mentoring and counseling. I've hired several mentors over the years who have impacted my life in very powerful ways.

The Bible tells us that there's wisdom in the counsel of many. It also says that a cord of three strands isn't easily broken. Having good influences will impact your ability to improve and grow. It's important to have people to speak hard truths into our lives. I love this quote by Trent Shelton – it pretty much sums up why we need to unpack the painful hurts from our past and put them into the right perspective:

> *"If you carry bricks from your past relationship to your new one, you'll only build the same house. Don't let the heart that is meant to love you suffer because of the heart that cared nothing about you."*[4]

Let's be honest; how you think about yourself and who you are is based upon what people have told you. This has a very significant impact upon your life and how you make decisions. How you think about yourself will make all the difference in how you look at the world. How you see the world will change how you think it sees you. How you believe the world sees you will cause you to act in certain ways. Sometimes this can be good – other times it has a very damaging and limiting effect upon your life. So many times, your thoughts will hinder you from the very things you've been created to do.

Stop and Reflect

- What untruths are you battling because of what someone once said to you?

- What have you been unable to do because prisoners of another mind in your past said that you couldn't?

- Have you tried to prove them wrong? Or did you prove them right by doing nothing?

Have faith that there's more; when you don't give up, you get more. Even the Bible says that after you've suffered for a little while, the God of all grace will restore and strengthen you. The most important part is that you must endure. We can't give up!

In conclusion, what other people might think about you isn't as important as what you think about yourself. When you learn to see yourself the way God sees you, you'll be able to do all the things He said you would be able to!

If we don't take a deeper look at ourselves, nothing will change.

Stop and Reflect

- Are you unwilling to deal with what happened in the past because it hurts too much? How has that past pain affected your life?

- How do you see God in your life? Are you angry at Him for not fixing life's broken areas?

- Do you do things that frustrate others because you want their attention? (This can be a hard one to admit, but it's very important for us to be honest.)

- In your life, who gives you solid advice? Are you listening?

- How do you see your self-worth? Upon what do you think your worth is based?

- In what ways have you cried out for help? Do you feel that they've fallen upon deaf ears?

She Never Felt Loved

She barely even gave it a second thought as her father walked past her – barking out orders and insults – to get into his truck to leave. She knew that saying anything would invite more shame – or even a beating, like so many times before. She simply turned away so that she wouldn't have to see the look of disgust upon his face.

Every day, she was criticized and mocked; it seemed that she could do nothing right – no matter how hard she tried. As the years passed, her heart became numb to her father and the people around her. She even gave up hope that he would call her by her real name instead of the nickname she hated so much!

Growing up, all she ever felt was the bitterness of his wrath. Many times, she wondered why she was even born. If they didn't want her, why didn't they just leave her at the hospital? Even with this thought, she feared that one day they *would* leave her and never come back. As the years passed, she imagined that maybe their life would be better without her. Maybe she would die, and they would be relieved because she wouldn't be a problem anymore. She wondered if they would be happy if she died; would they miss her? Or would they have a party because she was gone?

She carried many of these struggles into her adult life. She didn't realize that it shaped her thoughts and feelings for years to come. Like so many others, she didn't know that the harsh words spoken by her father would leave such long-lasting emotional scars.

I wish I could tell you that this is a made-up story; unfortunately, it's a true story. It's all too common. I've heard and seen these heartbreaking stories over and over. I've mentored and coached people from many different places around the world – with many diverse backgrounds. I see the same problem all over the world. I haven't yet seen a culture that isn't affected by this issue of the absent or abusive father. All too many of these girls will never hear words of encouragement from their fathers and will take their bitterness and resentment to their graves. How tragic it is that so many girls will grow up and live their whole lives without ever hearing a father figure say "I love you" or "I bless you, my daughter"!

Just as sad is the little girl that grew up with the hard-working father. While he provided a house, food, and clothing for his family, he didn't understand that his lack of affection caused his daughter to look for affection from others – from men – in other unhealthy places.

Have you felt the sting of rejection by your father? Are you like the little girl that wished she would just die – thinking that her family would be happier without her? Are you like so many other women and girls who have never heard your father say "I love you" or "I bless you, my daughter"? The girl in the story approached her father as an adult to put the pain of rejection behind her; she asked him to bless her. He mocked her instead. Is this something you can relate to? Have you tried to make things right with your father when he was unwilling to share love or affirmation with you?

Maybe you're like the daughter who wondered why her daddy was too tired to play with her after working all the time. You may have felt afraid to share how lonely you felt – everyone told you that he *needed* to work hard to get you the things you enjoy. Or maybe you felt guilty – that it was your fault that he worked so much. You would've been happy with fewer things if you could just spend more time with him. Was your father simply unable to share his affection with you because he was emotionally overwhelmed himself?

If you can relate in any way, this book was written to help set you free from the bondage of rejection. You're worthy to be blessed; you don't need to go another day without receiving a blessing from a father. This book was written to bless every woman and girl who doesn't feel loved or blessed by their father. Words that are spoken have the power to destroy – as well as the power to restore. I hope to speak to your heart and restore love and hope. Take these words from my heart to yours. As you read this book and receive this blessing into your heart, your life will never be the same.

Stop and Reflect

- If you can still hear a mocking, bitter voice – even many years after you've left your father – what feelings does it bring up? What do you feel it says about you?

- What are some of the things you wanted your father to say and do in your childhood that he didn't?

- Was your father the hard worker that was never there? If so, what are some of the negative feelings you had about him as a child?

- Have you tried to bury the pain of your father's absence by saying that he did all he could to provide for his family? Though that may be the truth, what kinds of feelings of loss or abandonment have you experienced from his absence?

- If your father was the one who didn't take the time to say "I love you," what impact did that have upon you as a child?

- What (incorrect) narrative did you tell yourself about why your father was working so hard? For example, did you feel that his life would be better if you were gone or had never been born? Did you feel like you were a burden?

He Didn't Know How to Love

In this chapter are some things that will hopefully help you to see life from a new perspective. To change your life forever, you must take a strong stand. This chapter will help you better understand why some people haven't been able to do what they should've done for you.

The one thing that's helped me be successful as a personal transformation coach is to help people get back to the basics before dealing with what's happening now. Everything has a beginning or a root – a place where it all started. It's my desire to help you break free from the pain and bondage you carry from not feeling loved by your father. I want to unpack some deeper truths about life and why people do what they do.

58

In all my years of mentoring, mission trips, and now being a personal transformation coach, I've seen a prevalent problem everywhere I go: The lack of a father's involvement with his children. Many fathers who think they love their children and completely miss the mark – and others don't care or even try to hit the mark. Too many fathers get so wrapped up in themselves that they have no idea what or how they're doing – let alone how their children are doing.

So many fathers fall into the trap of thinking that money and objects will show how much they love their children. Sadly, money and objects will never buy the love and affirmation we all need. Love isn't measured by how many gifts we give; it's measured by how much of ourselves we give!

One of my favorite sayings is: "*Everyone you meet is fighting a battle you know nothing about; show them some love.*"

Love can't be measured by what we buy for someone. That would mean that if you don't have money, you can't show how much you love someone. Everyone needs a little more (and at times, a lot more) love to make it to the next day. I want to give you that extra love. I want to help fill that empty void in your heart by blessing you and lifting you up to be the woman you were meant to be!

The greatest tragedy in the world isn't war or famine. I believe it's the lack of a father's love for his children. If fathers did their parts to love their children, there would be far less trouble in the world today. The statistics about children of fathers who aren't present are staggering. The rates of drug use, criminal activity, and school dropouts increase significantly when a father isn't involved in his child's life. See the Appendix for the tragic statistics related to fatherless homes.

We're all designed to give and receive love. When we don't get the love we should've gotten as a child, we have a love deficit – and a love deficit doesn't just go away on its own. A love deficit can easily stay with someone their whole life. The worst part is that the person may not even be aware of it. All too many times, they blame others for how they feel. They say that they wouldn't be like this if others would treat them better.

Maybe you've felt the sting of rejection from your father. Perhaps you're like me and grew up without a father in your home. Or maybe you had a father who was so wrapped up in his work that he didn't have time for you. Many people are simply broken and don't have anything to give. Can you imagine asking someone to get you a cup of water when all they have is a cracked, broken cup? Broken and empty people can't give you something they don't have.

Broken people look for others to complete them. Too many times, they find another broken person who's good at hiding their brokenness – until the demands upon them become too challenging and their brokenness gets exposed.

Depending upon the situation, they either become very depressed or very angry. Both are unhealthy ways to avoid dealing with the problem.

Now you have two empty and broken people – each demanding that the other one gives what they don't have. Neither can provide what the other needs because they have nothing to give. The more one thinks the other needs to lift them up, the more the other will demand the same. As you can imagine, it becomes an endless battle – one broken person breaking the other broken person down even more. When one demands that the other must change to become better, they give themselves a life sentence of misery.

Most people have a natural expectation that their father will give them love and meet their needs for affection, affirmation, and encouragement. This is how God meant it to be. But if your father was one of these broken people, he didn't have that love to give. In fact, he likely did the opposite. He likely made unrealistic demands and broke down the people he should have lifted up and loved the most… Including you.

When someone doesn't feel loved and deals with feelings of rejection, they stop trusting other people. As much as they desire to be loved and wanted, they build walls – safeguarding their heart to prevent people from hurting them again. These people have what we call an "Orphan's Heart." Their hearts are so closed and shut down that they can't give or receive

62

love. A person with an "Orphan's Heart" is not an evil person who tries to cause harm to others. They're just a hurt person – trying to protect their heart from getting hurt again. When someone is hurt over and over, they go to extreme lengths to make sure that no one will ever hurt them again.

As mentioned earlier, every person we meet is fighting a battle we know nothing about. It's important to remember that one person's struggles are as hard as another person's – just different. The pain of what we face hurts as much as the pain someone else struggles with. If it were easy, it wouldn't be a struggle. Some people are very good at hiding what they've been through – others can't hide anything. In the end, each person must take control of how they think and how they see the world. You can never become a better person or improve your life by demanding that someone else act or speak the way you want them to.

Stop and Reflect

- What does the love deficit in your own life feel like?

- In which (wrong) places are you looking for something to fill your love deficit? This might include bad relationships, addictions, over-working, trying to prove your worth, or possessions (your car, money, etc.). Do you have peace?

- Who are the broken and empty people in your life from whom you've been seeking love and affirmation?

- Write down some incidents when the love you didn't receive as a child felt like a reflection upon you and your worth. Do you feel that this could instead be a reflection upon those who couldn't give you that love?

- Do you still feel the pain of rejection, mockery, abandonment, or anything else from your childhood? What are some of the most painful memories and feelings?

- Do you think you might be ready to forgive your "broken" father for what he couldn't give? What do you need to forgive him for doing or not doing?

Counterfeit Affection

Over the years, I've gotten a deeper understanding of other people's struggles and how they deal with life. One of the ways people try to deal with life is with counterfeit affections. I believe that most people struggle with this – without even knowing! A counterfeit affection can be anything – from an unhealthy coping mechanism to a full-blown addiction – that's used to fill a place of emptiness in your heart. Counterfeit affections are specifically *unhealthy* ways of filling this emptiness. They're destructive to your soul – your mind, will, and emotions – and will leave you even more empty and broken; they can't deal with the root of the problem. When you come up empty, you often try to find other counterfeit affections to fill the void.

If you don't do what's right – no matter how hard – you can never be what you were designed to be. Hard times build the foundations of what you become. When you build your foundation upon anything counterfeit, it can't last. So the question is this: Why don't more people find success –

defined as "the progressive realization of a worthy goal"? Pursuing counterfeit affection is the death blow to finding success and fulfillment. It's just as important to understand the root of the problem as it is to understand what the problem is. People don't see this and so many other dream-crushing challenges because they're at the root of their being – they're looking at the fruit, trying to change things from the outside. You can paint an orange with green paint, but it will still taste like an orange.

Almost all our failures and successes stem from our roots. The seeds planted in your life will spring up and grow into huge trees that will bear fruit based upon the seed that was planted. Sounds simple enough, right?

The challenge is to look at the root of the problem. Counterfeit affection, negative speech, worrying, and fear are only a few of the issues that have deep roots.

What happens when you
do not deal with the problem

The good news is that when you start to break the
stranglehold they have on you, you see other problems you
may have. Counterfeit affection is deceiving and artificial. It
keeps you from finding real love and peace. Roger Taylor's
book *Love Hunger – The Unseen Force*[1] and Jack Frost's book
Spiritual Slavery to Spiritual Sonship[2] say that this comes from
an unmet love need. Counterfeit affection happens when
someone whose "love tank" is empty tries to fill someone
else's empty love tank – or when the tank is filled by

something else.

When your love need is from your father or mother (one seed that springs up and produces fruit), you seek other ways to fill it. This could be via addictions or compulsions to alcohol, drugs, food, promiscuity, adultery, or pornography – among other things. This hinders your ability to have a wholesome relationship with anyone because you're dividing your affection.

When your passion isn't filled in the proper way, you seek out other ways that are unhealthy in a spiritual, physical, or mental way. You develop bad habit structures that affect your life. None of them bring lasting satisfaction; they only give you a temporary fix. Some people work harder and harder all their lives to get more and more – but they never have enough. So many of them are never truly able to find real peace and happiness. The real problem is that they're trying to prove to someone (most times, their father) that they're good enough. They're really looking for their father to say "good job" or "I'm proud of you." Some people carry that burden to their grave – never truly understanding that unhealed hurts from the past drive them.

Making more money has become an acceptable counterfeit affection. Everyone says, "Wow, look at how well they're doing!" The rest of the family suffers because they're driven to work harder and harder – to make more and more.

When a parent doesn't receive affection from their spouse, they often seek counterfeit affection from their children. Loving your children is very important, but the wrong order of importance can be very unhealthy for both of you. When the parent receives love from their child – rather than their spouse – they won't find the root of the problem with their spouse. Because your spouse is a very important part of you, it's much easier to move forward when you help them stand on their feet.

When your unmet need is affection or attention, you may try to jockey for position. The need to be in control and to be the leader will never bring satisfaction – it's only a temporary fix for the real problem. Too many times, this turns into a demand that people respect us because we have position and power – but people won't respect the demands made upon them. They only do what's required of them until the demand is gone. Then they revert to what they did before. They never actually love the person that demands it – and that's why it can never be fulfilling.

70

If the need for love is for safety and security, you might fall into the trap of wanting more material things to feel secure. You may never feel satisfied with what you have and want more things to fill the emptiness. More is never enough – it won't matter how much you have. You can't find satisfaction in more.

All of the above counterfeit affections didn't grow overnight, and they won't be corrected overnight. The first step is the same as it is with every problem. You must admit that you have a problem. The second step is the willingness to do something about it. Everyone has struggles – most people are good at hiding them. The biggest problem is when you are unwilling to change. The fear of not getting more makes you dive deeper into what you shouldn't have – counterfeit affections. Often people convince themselves that counterfeit affection is the only thing that will make them happy – therefore, they *must* have it. If you don't allow yourself to pursue other interests that might be healthier, this can become a vicious cycle. You can never find real success and fulfillment if you don't let go of your unhealthy addictions. Take inventory of your life and see where you may have counterfeit affections keeping you from true joy and peace.

What is money and fame without true peace and joy? You don't need to look far to know that money can't buy real love or peace and lasting joy. Let me take a little liberty and say that Whitney Houston, Amy Winehouse, Elvis Presley, Marilyn Monroe, and many more are proof that fame and fortune don't bring lasting joy. True peace and joy can only come when you deal with the void in your life. If you have enough money to live comfortably but still aren't content, more money or fame won't change anything.

It's only by looking at the root of the problem that you're able to deal with it. Most times, you must go all the way back to your childhood to find the real issues. Most people don't want to do this because it brings up the painful memories they're trying to hide. This book is to help you deal with one of the deepest pains anyone can carry with them – not feeling love or acceptance from your father. My greatest desire is to never leave anyone the way I found them. I want to make them better by helping them think.

Stop and Reflect

- Do you feel like your love tank is empty? Which counterfeit affections are you using in an attempt to fill your tank?

- Do you find yourself turning to alcohol, drugs, food, sex, adultery, or pornography? Has that worked?

- Do you feel like you must always do more to be good enough? How has that affected you?

- Do you feel the need to be in control? What has that done to your relationships?

- Do you demand that people respect you? To what does that lead?

- Are you willing to take a step back and look at the root of the problem?

The Orphan's Heart

No matter where you go, you'll deal with people who have Orphan's Hearts. I want to help you understand what makes them act the way they do. That way, you'll be able to respond in a way that won't hurt you.

A person with an Orphan's Heart is not a child in a faraway country without a family. An Orphan's Heart is a heart that's emotionally and spiritually closed. The Orphan's Heart shuts down when a person doesn't feel loved and accepted by their parents (or people in positions of authority over them in the formative years of their life). Some people allow their hearts to close as they get older. Yes, I did say "*allow* their hearts to close." When a child closes their heart, it's because they don't know anything else. When an adult closes their heart, it's a *choice*. A child is still learning and forming their understanding of the world around them. An adult is not.

The lack of a father's love and attention is one of the biggest causes of an Orphan's Heart. If the child perceives that they weren't loved, their heart will close. We need to understand that perception becomes truth until the person is convinced otherwise. When a child believes they aren't loved or feels rejected by their earthly father, they struggle greatly with love from God – their Heavenly Father – as well. The more rejected they feel, the harder it is for the child to lay down their pride and forgive.

Pride and offense are some of the biggest stumbling blocks that the enemy uses to keep people from walking in God's truth and freedom. Because of pride, so many people go their whole lives with sadness and bitterness in their hearts. They never know the peace of walking in freedom. They never have joy in their hearts.

Satan became the first orphan when he was cast out of Heaven. Because he was thrown out by the Father, his desire is to make everyone an orphan as well. He knows that if he can keep people from knowing the true love of Father God, they won't be free.

A person that grows up in a loving, caring home can have an Orphan's Heart – every one of us has thought at one time or another that we weren't treated well or that we didn't receive the attention or affection we should have. Can you imagine a person who was mistreated in their childhood? Can you imagine how their heart would close because of abuse and neglect?

When a person has a love deficit that isn't filled with appropriate love or affection, their heart stays closed. The

reason this is such a big problem is because when the heart is

closed to *anyone*, it's closed to *everyone* – including God. When a person's heart is closed, they have a harder time hearing God. They don't believe that God even wants to talk to them. God can't pour out His anointing upon an   orphan because the orphan will only give when there's something they can get out of it. The orphan doesn't believe that there will be enough, so they take all they can and won't share.

A heart of love will give until it stops beating, and that's why God will only pour out His greatest anointing upon a heart filled with love.

Interestingly, the Orphan's Heart will amplify the personality of the individual. A person who's naturally driven will try to prove to the world (mostly their father) that they do things just as well as – or better than – others, and they become very successful in most of what they do. On the opposite side, you have a person who's naturally emotional. They can be driven into deep, long-lasting depression, and they may struggle to cope with life. These two are the extremes of what can happen. There's everything in between – from hyper-religious people to leeches who refuse to stand on their own and will suck you dry before they move on to the next. One thing is certain: No matter if they hide their Orphan's Heart, they'll stop at nothing to protect what they have. They'll fight to the bitter end to stay on top.

The heart of love is only proven by the hurt it will endure. Allow me to unpack this a bit more: Let's say you're using a chain to lift something up. As you're lifting it up, the chain breaks. Did the whole chain fail, or did just one part fail?

Only one part failed – which caused the whole operation to fail. A chain is only as strong as its weakest link. The whole chain could be made of the highest grade of steel, but if one link isn't as high a quality as the others, the whole operation fails.

When we're unable to forgive the ones that hurt us – no matter what they did – we can't walk in full love and freedom. When we allow the pain and rejection of the past to drag us down, it destroys us – and this becomes the weakest link. The bondage of the past drives us to seek unhealthy relationships or act in unhealthy ways. The only way to walk in peace and freedom is to reconcile our past. We must put all things into perspective by understanding the truth about who we are.

It's important to look at the truth of who you are now – not who someone said you were in the past. You must look at the truth of who you are based upon what you do and think right now. No one is still who they were in their past; everyone changes.

Real, true freedom can only happen when you forgive those who weren't there for you. People likely hurt you very badly in the past. I can't imagine the pain you're carrying. I'll say it again; the only way to true freedom is to forgive. When you don't forgive and let go, you only hurt yourself. You allow that person to live in your head and control you. Being angry and unforgiving is like drinking poison and hoping the other person dies. The other person moves on with their life, and you still suffer – because you haven't stopped holding on to it.

The next step is to understand if you have – or if your father has – an Orphan's Heart. This can lead to forgiveness. A lack of forgiveness can even affect your physical body and be the cause of major problems in your life.

An Orphan's Heart – or orphan's spirit – is characterized by a feeling of not belonging. It carries with it a deep-seated sense of not being accepted, valued, honored, or loved.

"If a child does not acquire self-confidence from their parents, it is unlikely they'll ever possess self-confidence as adults. Conversely, if a child does gain it in childhood, it is unlikely that anything in adulthood will discourage them." – M. Scott Peck[3]

"It causes one to live life as if he does not have a safe and secure place in the Father's heart. He feels he has no place of affirmation, protection, comfort, belonging or affection. Self-oriented, lonely and inwardly isolated, he has no one from whom to draw Godly inheritance." – Jack Frost[2]

Let's take a deeper look at how an orphan acts out and some things to be aware of. Listed below are some traits you may see in yourself or others who may have an Orphan's Heart:

- They're very performance oriented.

- They would rather have rules than relationships.

- They have a fear-based theology rather than grace and mercy.

- They feel that God doesn't love or care about them – even though they believe the Bible to be the truth.

- They find it very difficult to maintain close relationships.

- They hold on to offenses and show conditional love.

- They blame others for things that happen and don't like to be held responsible.

- They run away from problems.

- They reject authority.

- They don't trust others and feel that they don't belong.

- They exhibit envy or anger and want to control everything.

- They feel condemnation and shame.

- They desire the praise of other people and want to be seen for what they do.

- They're very critical of other people.

You can likely think of someone that fits into this category. Some of these things might be in our own hearts as well. Any person uncomfortable with love is not healed. Many people hide the truth of how badly they're hurting. Some people hide it by working. We say, "Look at them; they're working so hard and doing so well." The real question is this: Why are they working so hard? What are they trying to prove? So many people try to prove to their fathers that they're worthy by working harder. They say, "That's just the way I am," when the real issue is that they want others to see their hard work and accomplishments.

There are far too many people who hide the pain in alcoholism, food, drugs, or sex. Others don't hide it at all; they just become depressed or aggressive and violent. They display their hurt with outbursts of anger, sadness, and depression.

More and more, doctors try to fix people with medication – when it's actually an emotional problem that stems from deeply rooted beliefs. A person with an Orphan's Heart can't feel love; they only look for what they can get from a relationship. Please understand that they aren't bad people. They don't simply want to do what's wrong. The orphan operates out of fear. Because they don't believe they'll receive anything, they take everything they can get. No matter how much they get, they still don't believe they'll have enough to survive – so they need to take more and more… And still they'll never get enough.

On a side note, orphans never share what they have with others. I know of a lady who adopted an 18-month-old child from a Russian orphanage. She watched the child very closely – the girl took dog food and hid it in her pant legs, afraid she wouldn't have enough to eat later. If this happens with an 18-month-old child, imagine what happens if this belief isn't corrected by the time someone reaches their 20s, 30s, or older.

The orphan won't give unless they know they'll get something in return. They can't love – they've been so wounded that they feel it's unsafe to take a chance on love.

Their fear of rejection is so great that they would rather live without love than take a chance and be rejected or hurt again. Orphans turn to anger to protect themselves. Anger is control. It's a way to control fear. When someone is afraid, they often use anger to regain control. Perfect love casts out fear – in other words, perfect love casts out anger.

Keep in mind that a person who knows a great deal about scripture or can memorize a great number of verses isn't necessarily a healed and whole person. Just because a person is a great leader and people love them, that doesn't mean they're healed.

Many powerful leaders achieve their positions because they're driven by fear or feelings of insignificance. They climb the ladder to be seen and to prove their worth. The problem is that when everyone has seen what they've done and the pats upon the back cease, they need to do something else to get their approval fix – just like a drug addict. So many great leaders in business and ministry build their successes at the cost of their family. Their families have paid the price of a father seeking worthiness for his performance – and not for the value of being a father.

In these cases, it's important to know that it wasn't your fault; he was broken and didn't have anything to give you. He was so empty that all he could do was look for his next fix – his next affirmation from others.

You can't take responsibility for the wrong actions of other people. If you want to walk in freedom, you must understand that you didn't cause them to turn away from you. They made a choice – they didn't have the emotional strength to deal with their struggles. It wasn't your fault. They were empty before you met them.

Stop and Reflect

- Have you struggled with any of the traits of the orphan? Do you believe your father may struggle (or has struggled) with any of the traits? Ask yourself why you have (or he has) that trait. Remember: Not dealing with any of these areas will make it difficult to open your heart to healing. Also, recognizing these traits in your father may help you realize why he couldn't give you what he didn't have and – ultimately – forgive him.

- Did you suffer as your absent father became successful?

- Did you feel like the second-hand doll that was tossed aside?

- Did you feel abandoned as you watched your father chase his dreams?

The Power of Forgiveness

This is one of the most important chapters to understand – it will affect everything about your life. A lack of forgiveness has the power to destroy everything in your life and leave you in ruins. Every war ever fought started with the lack of forgiveness.

If you allow it to go unchecked, unforgiveness can – and will – destroy your physical body, consume your soul, and destroy your life. I want to help you understand what forgiveness is and what forgiveness isn't. It doesn't put any shame or guilt upon you or force you to be involved with unsafe people.

Many people suffer because they don't understand what forgiveness is. They have the wrong idea of what it means to forgive and what's expected after they forgive. Forgiving simply means that you consciously and deliberately make a choice to release any and all feelings of resentment, anger, or bitterness toward a person who hurt you – no matter if they deserve it.

In other words, you no longer require them to repay you a debt. It would be like someone borrowing $100 from you. Eventually, they say, "I'm sorry. I can't pay you the $100. I don't have it." If you decide that they don't need to pay you back, you would respond, "I'll forgive your debit; you no longer owe me the money." Forgiving the debt means that you forfeit the right to demand they repay you the money. It has been forgiven.

Forgiving Isn't the Same as Forgetting

You can't make yourself forget things done to you. Just because you've forgiven someone of their debt doesn't mean you forgot what they borrowed. This is where the problem lies. We hear all too many people say, "Forgive and forget." But you can't force yourself to forget about something that happened to you.

Everything that happens is imprinted upon your brain – including what you think and feel. Every time something similar occurs, the event in the past will be part of the new conclusion you come to.

Every moment of every day, your brain does research to determine what will happen next – based upon the meaning you give to similar events in your past. Because you're the sum of all your parts, every part of your past will determine what you think about your future – unless you change the meaning you've given to past events.

Forgiveness doesn't necessarily change what happened or make you responsible for it. It changes the fact that you no longer want payback for what happened. You're releasing the offender from the burden of doing anything for you in return.

When you hold unforgiveness, bitterness, strife, anger, hate, resentment, revenge, etc. against someone, every time you think of them, your mind immediately focuses on what they did. When your mind's space is partially or totally taken over by what happened, you're no longer able to use your brain for other productive thoughts. Imagine that you allow this to happen a lot – you lose time thinking about something you can't change... And that time is gone forever.

When you lose time, you never get it back again – it's gone. The time you spend reading this book is gone forever. No matter how hard you try, you can't buy one second back. For this reason, time is more important than money. If you lose $1,000, you can work hard and earn the money back – not so with time.

When you lose time by thinking about how bad your situation is and how someone hurt you, it takes up your brain's space and time. You'll never be able to get it back again – no matter what you do. It's gone forever! Forgiveness frees up your mind's space. It never makes you forget what happened. You simply think about it in a different way – a way that doesn't steal your peace, joy, or precious time.

Forgiveness doesn't mean that they were right and that you were wrong.

When you forgive someone, it doesn't mean what they did was right or acceptable. You're in no way condoning what they did – nor are you giving them permission to do it again. Likewise, your forgiveness doesn't mean you have to allow them to be part of your life again.

When you forgive someone, you aren't taking responsibility for what they did. You're simply not demanding that they owe you. Forgiveness lets them go and releases them from the burden of doing anything for you in return.

Let me stress again that when you forgive someone, you aren't justifying what they did – nor are you taking the blame for what they did. Wrong is wrong – regardless of whether you decide to hold it against them or let it go.

Forgiveness Doesn't Allow Anyone to Hurt You Again

When you forgive someone, you aren't giving them permission to be in your life again. Forgiveness simply releases them from owing you something. There's nothing about forgiveness that allows them to be part of your life again if you feel unsafe. It also means that you don't have to interact with them – period. Forgiveness isn't a ticket for anyone to ride your train.

Let me say that again: Forgiving someone doesn't mean you must see them, talk to them, or interact with them ever again – period. There are many people that I've honestly forgiven, yet I have no desire to deal with them. What happened is in the past – I simply have no desire to be part of their lives – nor do I want them to be part of mine. They don't need me, and I don't need them. That isn't to say that forgiveness can never include the restoration of a relationship with safe boundaries. Sometimes people change. There may be a reason you want to spend time with them again.

The key here is true forgiveness. If you haven't sincerely forgiven them, unforgiveness will take up space in your brain – it only hurts you in the long run. Often, the person will never know that you remember what happened and that you're holding it against them. They're fighting their own battles – battles that have nothing to do with you.

If you feel unsafe or don't trust someone, you shouldn't force yourself to be around them – even if you've forgiven them. If you want to live a whole and complete life, you need to protect yourself first.

Unforgiveness Will Destroy Your Body

How you think and what you think about has a direct effect upon your physical health. I strongly believe that this information should be part of the curriculum throughout schooling. Understanding emotional awareness is a much bigger factor in your success than culture, social connections, wealth, or demographics. This is a powerful and fascinating field of study.

Science has proven many times that thoughts have a direct effect upon the cellular functions of your body – how and what we think about can cause sickness. Check the References section for a few researchers in this field that I highly recommend. They all have a lot of powerful and amazing content online that you can review for free. I highly recommend that you take some time to get a basic understanding of what they're teaching – it's life-changing!

The Positive Power of Forgiveness

When I was in the sign-building business, I had a competitor who would tell my customers anything to convince them not to hire me. He even went so far as to beg a customer to hire anyone else – just so they wouldn't hire me. For that reason, I lost several jobs to him over the years.

I can't say that this didn't hurt – I helped him in many ways and looked at him as a friend. I never hated him for what he did. I knew what was happening deep in his heart and mind. He had always been a bully; he pushed his way around to get what he wanted.

One day, I found out that – once again – he had bad-mouthed me about a job upon which both of us bid. I decided that I'd had enough and went to his shop. I told him that if I ever heard that he was spreading rumors about me again, I would go to his shop every day and pray for him. If he didn't allow me in the shop, I would stand outside – facing his security camera – and pray for him.

I could easily have sued him and won; he did this many times – and to many people. But how would that have helped me in the long run? It would've made him angry, and he would've done it again – if not to me, then to others. I'm sure he said more bad things about me, but after I visited him, I never heard about it again. That visit released me from feeling angry or bitter toward him. While I did lose income to him, forgiving him freed my brain's space – it allowed me to focus on other things.

Today he still struggles to keep employees and doesn't enjoy his life. I still stop by to see him and talk to him – even after he treated me so unfairly. He never dealt with the real problem – one that has nothing to do with me. This is a perfect example of what a lack of forgiveness will do to your mind and heart.

The Destructive Power of Unforgiveness

When you don't clear your mind of the things that hurt you in the past, it will become part of what hurts you in the future. The anger and bitterness that this man directed at me was there long before I came into his life. I simply became the new target for his old, festering anger.

When people are angry, they often blame other people for their suffering. No one made them angry; they've just found a new target to release what was already there. If they don't change how they think about the first time they felt this anger, nothing will change.

Finding the root of your anger is the key to healing your heart. The memories of past wrongs become the vessels for anger and bitterness – they're poured out upon anyone who stumbles into that minefield. I encourage you to let go of the past by changing its meaning. When you understand that those who hurt you were simply broken and empty, they didn't know how to be kind, it can help you let go of past hurt. Knowing this will help you forgive them.

Never forget: You can't be angry and happy at the same time. Both are a choice, and you're the only one that can give meaning to anything. The meaning you give to something is up to you. Please choose wisely.

Stop and Reflect

- Is your brain power being wasted with unforgiveness?

- Do you get a sense of satisfaction in knowing that you're holding a grudge?

- Are you afraid that if you forgive, they'll be allowed to hurt you again?

- Do you think that forgiving is letting someone off the hook?

- Can you see how unforgiveness is only hurting you – and no one else?

- Are you ready to walk away from your mental prison?

- Are you ready to forgive yourself?

Why Do I Need a Father's Blessing?

You aren't wasting your time reading this book. If you read this whole book and open your heart to receive it, you'll never be the same. The only thing I ask is that you give me a chance to share a blessing with you – from my heart to your heart. Lay down any anger, fear, or doubts you may be holding on to in your heart. This may be asking a lot from you, and it won't be easy. I struggled almost all my life without trusting anyone. I lost out on a lot because I feared people would abuse me again. All I ask is that you take a chance and open your heart to hear what I share – and allow it to touch your heart. If you do, your life will never be the same again!

This is a process. This isn't a magical book that will change your life just because you read it. You'll have to do the hard work; this book and the Father's Blessing are powerful tools, but they can't do more than you allow them to! The rest of this book won't mean anything if you don't follow the steps. It's not a bad idea to read through this several times. Each time, you'll be able to see things you didn't see the first time. Each time, you'll be a new person – able to see it in a different way.

Everyone has a sincere desire to hear their father's words of approval; every little girl wants to know that she's loved and wanted by her father. We all know the sad truth of absent fathers and the adverse effect they have upon our world. But there's hope for all those that missed out on the feeling of being wanted by a daddy who loved and blessed them. The deep wounds that many people work so hard to bury or brush aside can be healed. Many people search in all the wrong places to fill the void that can only be filled with a father's love.

I've heard many people say that they restored their relationship with their fathers as they got older. When I ask if they ever appropriately dealt with what happened in their childhood, the majority admitted that they had not. They weren't willing to get closure because they were afraid to feel the pain again. Most people are unaware that the pain didn't go away just because they achieved a better relationship with their father as an adult. The pain of loss doesn't go away when you don't talk about it. If you don't face the past and deal with it, it will always be there. No matter how much you try to hide it, it will become part of your future.

It's essential to understand that you're the sum of all your parts – everything in your past is part of you. If you never change the meaning you gave to something, the wrong meaning will always be part of who you think you are. While it's true that you can't change what happened in your past, you can change the meaning you give to it – that will change how you think and act in the future.

I want to help you rewrite the meaning you give your past. The focus of this book is to help you see that you're worthy of love and that you're blessed. When you rewrite the meaning of your life at its core, it will radically change how you think and act. This will change your life forever!

The blessing I've written in this book is from my heart – "the heart of a father" – to share with women and girls who didn't feel loved by their father. When you open your heart and receive this blessing, it will fill the void that wasn't adequately filled by your natural father. Over the years, I've stood in the place of many fathers and shared this blessing over thousands and thousands of people; I've seen firsthand the powerful transformation it had upon their lives. The words spoken by others have left wounds upon their lives. Now I want to share the powerful words of this blessing to help bring you healing.

I know the pain of abandonment. The cruel feelings of emptiness still haunt the shadows of my mind if I don't cast them down and take control of them. If I allowed them to run unchecked, these thoughts and feelings could be devastating to my soul.

Can you still hear his harsh words – cutting into the depth of your soul?

Do you long to hear words of affection and affirmation spoken to you?

Before I go on, let's dig a little deeper. Many people suffer needlessly because they're unwilling to deal with their past. I've seen countless people struggle to bury their feelings – so they don't have to deal with them. If you don't deal with your past, there's no peace and no joy. You can't out-work, out-drink, or out-spend the pain of your past. You must deal with them in the proper way and put them into perspective.

If your feelings of abandonment or rejection – no matter how small the reason – still hurt when you think about them, they aren't healed! **Feelings buried alive will never die**. If you don't deal with them properly, they become limiting burdens for the rest of your life. Holding on to a wrong belief can prevent you from living your life to the fullest. If you don't let go of the wrong thoughts or feelings about your past, you're the only one who suffers for it.

The Father's Blessing isn't the cure to all your problems. Regardless, the lack of a father's affection can have a devastating impact upon a child's life – one that many will carry to the grave. Receive this blessing and let go of whatever has weighed upon your heart and mind for all these years. Whatever it is – now is the time to let it go. Now is the time to receive the love of a father and know you're worthy and loved! Here's the key: Are you willing to take a chance and open your heart one more time?

A love deficit – a lack of real love – that isn't filled won't be healed. This blessing is written to share the love and affirmation you may have never heard. In this blessing, I stand in the place of your father and speak powerful words of affirmation and assurance. Spoken word has the power of life and death. The Father's Blessing has the power of life. When you receive this blessing into your heart, it transforms how you see yourself and the world around you.

This blessing won't take the place of what only Jesus Christ or the Holy Spirit can do; this blessing is only a way to help people tear down the walls in their hearts that stop them from walking in freedom.

Stop and Reflect

- How does it feel to take a chance and trust one more time – to open your heart to find what you've missed?

- Are you ready to face the pain from your past and open your heart to healing?

- What meaning have you given to the events that happened in your past? Can you envision the harm that the wrong meaning has caused?

- Would you like to change the meaning you've given to your past and to let go of the pain?

- As you look at what was broken in your past relationships, do you think you've merely covered it up? What could you do to handle the pain differently?

- Remember: If it still hurts when you think about it, then it's not healed. What events or situations in your past still cause you pain when you think about them?

Before You Read the Blessing

I'm so excited you're reading this book; when you open your heart and allow the truth of who you are fill and transform you, your life will never be the same! Here I'll explain how to have a much deeper experience with this blessing. I'll stand in the place of your father and share with you what so many people haven't heard from their fathers. No matter what happened in your past, I bless you as a daughter – because you're worthy to be blessed.

Before you read this blessing, prepare your heart and mind to fully receive the love I share with you. I strongly encourage you not to read the Father's Blessing until you have at least one or two hours to relax afterward. Turn off your phone, clear your schedule, and set time aside. This blessing isn't something you should read quickly before running back to your busy life. Allow this blessing to soak into your heart.

Read it over and over. Receive it into every part of your being. Take the time to hang on to every word I've written – I truly mean them.

I will this stress again: Please make time to receive this blessing. Make sure your phone is turned off, and let others know you won't be available for a couple of hours. Take the time to rest your heart and mind – allow this to fill your whole being. Block out a few hours to relax and soak in the new environment in which you find yourself. Allow every part of your mind and heart to absorb the blessing; allow it to transform every cell of your body! Know with all your being that you're truly worthy to be loved; you're wanted and are of great value!

I've shared the Father's Blessing with thousands of people over the years. I've seen firsthand the powerful transformation that takes place when people open their hearts and allow love to flow in. This blessing won't cure everything or fix all your struggles; it won't make all your problems go away. It's meant to break the chains of rejection from your father. Receive the affirmation you may have never received before – you're worthy to receive love and affirmation as a daughter. You're worthy to be loved and respected as a daughter. This blessing is meant to give you the courage and strength to take a firm stand – because you're powerful. This was written for you to know your value and stop your negative thinking; so you can believe in yourself again!

I want to be a spiritual father to you and bless you. Open your heart and trust that this is real. It's as real as the words you're reading right now. Once again, make sure you're in a quiet place where you won't be disturbed and that you have time to receive this blessing. Please don't be in a hurry to read through it and rush off. Take the time to fully bask in the blessing. Let it heal every wound and break every curse. Allow it to overpower all the negative thoughts and beliefs you've ever felt. As you allow this to break the lies from your past, focus on your new beliefs. Take all the time necessary.

I don't want you to be the same after you've read and received this blessing. My desire is that it will be completely life-changing!

Preparing for the Blessing (Optional)

Physical acts will help enhance this experience by making it more dramatic and impactful.

Get an old towel – preferably one you would be willing to throw away. If you don't have an old towel, you can use any piece of fabric. (In a pinch, even paper towels would work.) Make sure it's long enough to lay over both of your shoulders. Before you start to read, wrap it around your shoulders. At one point in the blessing, I'll tell you to take the towel off and throw it into the garbage. This is a physical act that helps bring closure and demonstrates that you're no longer allowing those issues in your life. It's a strong symbolic gesture of breaking off something you've carried with you.

If you need to do this multiple times, I encourage you to do so – if it will help you to walk in freedom, the cost of a towel is a very small price to pay. If you feel you're carrying a lot of shame or guilt, make sure to use several towels. You don't have to get this right the first time. Feel free to go through the blessing as many times as you need – until you feel you've been completely set free. Don't rush.

The most important part is to keep a positive and renewed mind after you break off all the negative feelings. This won't come naturally; you'll have to work at it. You'll have to make a conscious effort to think in a new way.

Next find a small wooden stick – like a paint-stirring stick, a pencil, or chopsticks. At one point, I'll instruct you to break the stick. This physical act helps to reinforce the words you're reading. You may want to use several sticks. Like before, place the broken sticks into the garbage. Doing this will help you create the physical sensation of breaking these blockages – your old way of thinking – from your life.

Do all this when you read the blessing. This is to make sure you've broken every chain binding you to your past wounds. This is to make sure you're free to become all you were created to be. If you have other objects you want to throw away, this is a good time to get rid of them. This will be a time of healing and a time to "clean your emotional house." Find any objects with ties to the person who hurt you. If an object brings painful memories, you may want to throw it away. Doing this can be a strong declaration that this person won't have power over you anymore. When you have all the items in the garbage bag, tie it closed with a knot. Then declare that everything in that bag is from your past and isn't part of your future.

After you tie it closed, take the bag out of the house. Doing so is a very powerful symbol that you've removed those roadblocks and your old way of thinking from your life. I would even recommend you drive somewhere else to dispose of it. Most gas stations have a trash can into which you can put things. Please don't litter; make sure that as you get rid of your burden, you aren't causing a problem for others.

Lastly get some anointing oil, if you do not have any you can make it yourself. Put a little bit of olive oil in a bowl and ask the Lord to bless it. Place it in one hand, hold your other hand over it, and repeat this prayer:

> "Father God, I ask You to bless this oil. Let Your mercy and goodness dwell in it. I pray that You bring healing and restoration to the body, soul, and spirit of the individuals who are anointed with this oil. Amen."

I wish I could be there in person to share this blessing with you. I hope we meet in person someday so I can give you a hug!

Read the blessing as many times as you need – until you feel you've dealt with all the areas in your life. If – at any time – you feel you haven't dealt with something, feel free to go back and do it again. You deserve to walk in the freedom of wholeness. You're worthy to be loved and blessed. There's a good chance you'll feel something change in this time. You may even feel like you're walking on air. You may feel like something has been lifted off you – like an oppressive spirit has left you.

You may feel things happening. Your heart may beat faster or skip a beat. In your mind, you may see a vision, an impression, or have a new thought. In your spirit, you may pick up on a new sense, vibe, or energy. In your body, you may experience tingling, heat, or goosebumps. All these things are good – they mean something new is happening within you! It's part of the miracle of this blessing!

Stop and Reflect

Here's a checklist of the items that can make this a more dramatic and impactful experience.

- An old towel, or paper towels

- Thin wooden sticks

- A garbage bag

- (Optional) Anointing oil

The Father's Blessing

I know you'll be blessed as you read this and take it into your heart. I affirm that you're worthy to receive the love I'm sharing here. Once again, I affirm that if you're reading this, this is for you. I love you – no matter what you do or don't believe. I love you and want to bless you – no matter what you've done. I'm not here to judge you for anything. You're worthy to be blessed and loved.

Place the towel around your shoulders. Now take a deep breath. Let your heart and mind relax as you take in these words.

The Apology

My daughter – as a spiritual father, I come to you with a humble and broken heart. I'm sorry for all the wrong things I did. I'm sorry I wasn't there for you when you needed me as a father – as a daddy.

It wasn't your fault in any way. It was out of the emptiness of my heart – out of my brokenness – that I couldn't give you more. I was the broken one who didn't do what I should've; it's my fault – not yours.

I'm sorry I didn't love you the way you needed to be loved. I'm sorry I didn't hold you as a little girl who needed her daddy. I was the foolish one who didn't know how to love you.

I'm so sorry I chose to go to work without stopping to spend time with you. I now see what I missed by not being there for you. I'm so sorry I didn't go to your events – that I didn't watch you perform or play sports.

I see now that I was wrong not to take the time to sit with you and help you with your homework or projects. I can't justify it; there's no excuse for not being there.

I'm sorry for the accusing words I spoke. You didn't do anything to deserve the harsh treatment you received. There's nothing you could've done to deserve being screamed at. I take back all the blame and shame I put upon you.

None of it was your fault. I was the one who was wrong – for not helping you in your time of need. I'm so sorry I yelled at you when you did things I didn't like. I regret that I didn't take the time to help you through your struggles.

I was wrong for not showing how much I loved you. I was wrong for not taking the time to comfort you as my daughter. There are so many things I did wrong, and I'm sorry; I'm the one who was at fault.

I'm so sorry for any time your punishment didn't fit what you did. I overstepped my bounds when I was harsh with you and made you suffer when your mistakes were minor.

My daughter, I'm so sorry I turned away from you and didn't listen to you. I may never agree with or understand some of the choices you've made. I may never agree with or understand what you do. But it was wrong for me not to listen and not to love you no matter what. I was wrong for cutting you out of my life because we didn't agree.

My love, it doesn't matter what you've done. Nothing makes it right for me to turn my back on you and push you out of my life. I'm so sorry; I was wrong.

I was so wrong for being a drunk or drug addict and not being a good role model for you and our family. I can't use the excuse that I had a hard life and that that's how I dealt with it. There's no reason I should've done what I did; I played the victim and put the blame upon others. I didn't stand up and face my problems.

I'm sorry I didn't support you and our family better. I'm sorry I didn't look for a better job to provide for our family. I can't express how sorry I am that I took your money because I didn't want to work. I was very wrong.

To anyone who was physically abused by their father, I'm so sorry for hitting or beating you; there's nothing you could've done to deserve being hit, punched, or kicked.

I was wrong – very wrong; it wasn't your fault. I take the blame for what I did. You didn't bring it upon yourself; you didn't deserve it.

My daughter, you never did anything – ever – that justified physical violence. You should never have been handled roughly or slapped for any reason. There's nothing you could have done to justify that.

I'm so sorry for hurting you like this; there's nothing that can justify treating you with disrespect. I'm the one who was out of control, and I take the blame for what I did. I'm sorry.

I didn't respond in the proper way when you did things I didn't approve of. I was wrong for not correcting you in a loving and respectful way. I take all the blame for hurting you. This should never have happened; I'm sorry – this wasn't your fault.

For anyone who lived in an oppressive home, I'm so sorry. I cannot express the grief it brings me to know that a father can beat or torture his family.

I condemn the mistreatment and abuse of others for any reason; there's never an excuse to physically, sexually, or mentally abuse or batter anyone – ever! To anyone who was mistreated by their father, I want to stand as a father and say that I'm sorry – it's very wrong! There's no way to justify abuse of any kind – ever!

For anyone who was sexually abused by their father – or any other person – I can't begin to understand the trauma this caused. I'll never know the pain you suffered or your trauma.

The severity of the abuse doesn't matter. It was wrong, and it wasn't your fault. It doesn't matter if you were curious and wanted to know more; they were the ones who were wrong. You can't carry the blame and shame for what someone should've protected you from.

I'm sorry for the ones that exposed themselves to you. That was very wrong, and you didn't invite or cause them to do that. It was out of the sickness in their minds.

All I can do is stand in the place of the offender and say, "I'm sorry. I'm so very sorry for what happened." There's no way being assaulted could've been your fault – this means everything from being touched to being raped. You didn't do anything to bring this upon yourself.

What happened was very wrong, and there's no way to excuse it. Let me take the guilt from you and cast it away from you.

I release you from the guilt and shame – even if you agreed to do something sexually, knowing it was wrong, to make the other person happy. They're the one who was wrong for making you feel obligated.

You can't take the blame for any of this – you didn't cause this to happen. You've been a victim of abuse, and you can't carry the shame or the guilt anymore!

Now is the time to throw off the guilt and shame you've been carrying. You didn't cause this to happen. Know very clearly that you didn't cause any of this.

Declaring freedom

Say the following aloud:

> "I will not carry the guilt, shame, condemnation, or fear for what [offender's name] did to me. I am free from the bondage [offender's name] held over me. I refuse to live in the shadows because [offender's name] [what they did]to me."

> "I am free of all the guilt, shame, condemnation, and fear; I declare that it does not have a hold on me anymore. I did not cause it, and I refuse to carry it anymore!"

> "I declare all the guilt, shame, condemnation, and fear has been cast down, and I will not carry it anymore!"

Add anything that you feel needs to be added.

Now take the towel on your shoulders and throw it in the garbage.

Take the stick and hold it in both hands – but don't break it until you have said the following:

"I break off the spirit of fear and unbelief."

"I break off the victim's spirit and the orphan's spirit that have taken me into bondage."

"I break off all the self-hate and condemnation I hold in my heart and mind."

"I break off all the spiritual ties I have from being sexually involved with anyone who is not my spouse."

"I break all the unhealthy emotional ties with these people."

Once again, add anything you feel needs to be added.

Now break the stick. Believe – in your heart – that the curse is broken and you're free from the bondage.

Don't skip this next step if you want to walk in freedom. Invite the Holy Spirit of God to come and fill every part of your heart and mind. Ask Him to come and complete the cleansing of your soul, and then invite Him to fill every part of your being. Here's a sample prayer:

> "Holy Spirit, I invite You to come and fill every empty place in my heart and soul. I ask You to search me and show me any place that is unclean. Help me to see anything that still needs to be broken. I ask You to search my heart and soul and restore everything that is missing. I ask You to repair everything broken and stand upright anything that has fallen. Wash me, cleanse me, and make me pure."

> "I ask You to give me the wisdom to know the next steps to take in my renewed life. I ask You to dwell in me and to show me the truth. I ask You to show me who I really am."

Be very aware of what you feel; do you feel completely free of the feelings of oppression and heaviness? If you don't, repeat this step as many times as you need – until you feel a sense of freedom. Now take the broken stick and throw it in the garbage. This is part of your past; it no longer has a hold upon you anymore. You're free! You're released from all responsibility for the wrongful actions of your father – no matter what. You never did anything to deserve any kind of abuse.

Take the garbage bag with the trash from the past and tie it shut. As you're tying it, say:

> "I bind all this on earth as it is in Heaven. I say that you, garbage, will have no power over me anymore. You must release me, and I forbid you to return. I forbid you to go to any of my family or friends."

You can download a copy of this from our website at *www.fathersblessing.info/resources.php* and clicking "**Declaring Freedom.**"

The Blessing

Now, my daughter, I bless you. Please receive this from my heart to your heart; you are worthy.

I bless the time of your conception with the Father's Blessing. You aren't a mistake. You aren't an accident. You're wanted as a daughter. I thank God for you.

I bless the first trimester in your mother's womb. I declare that you're wanted as a daughter. You're accepted, and you aren't rejected. You're loved and not cursed; you aren't a burden.

I bless the second trimester in your mother's womb. You're loved, and you aren't a mistake. You aren't a burden at all. You're wanted as a daughter, and you're a blessing. You aren't rejected, and you aren't abandoned.

I bless the third trimester in your mother's womb. You're loved as a daughter. You aren't a burden; you aren't a mistake. You're exactly the daughter I wanted. You aren't rejected; you aren't abandoned. I thank God for you.

I bless the day of your birth as a daughter. You aren't a problem, and you're wanted as a daughter. I bless you with the Father's Blessing.

I break any and all curses from you. I call your spirit to life as a daughter. I call you to rise up as a daughter – as a woman. There's no confusion in you; you're blessed to be a daughter.

No curse formed against you can prosper. I break the spirit of death. The slumbering spirit must release you. The spirits of bondage and fear – as well as all familiar spirits – must release you now in the name of Jesus.

I bless all the years of your childhood; I say that there are no wrong ways in you. You aren't a burden. You're wanted and loved. You aren't rejected, and you aren't abandoned.

I bless all your years as a teenager. I say that you aren't a burden and that there's no wicked way in you. You aren't rejected or abandoned; you're loved and accepted. You aren't too much to handle; you're wanted as a daughter.

I bless all your days as an adult; I say that you're loved as a daughter. You're wanted. You aren't rejected or abandoned; you're accepted. You're a very beautiful daughter, and I love you with all my heart.

I bless all the days of your life and declare that you're wanted as a daughter. You're loved. There's no rejection in you at all; I speak life into you – not curses. You're accepted.

I speak life into your soul – that you may rise up and not fall down.

I break off all shame you received or that you felt was put upon you. I release you of all guilt. I forgive you, and I speak all good blessings into you as a daughter. I call your spirit to life, breaking every curse for all wrongs.

In closing, take the anointing oil and put a dab upon your forehead as you read this aloud.

> "I, Papa Ray, declare that you, [your name], are worthy. I say that you, [your name], are holy. You're blessed, and you're wanted. [Your name], you're loved. I, Papa Ray Hurst, bless you, [your name], with the Father's Blessing. I bless you as a daughter. I love you forever."

After the Blessing

Take the trash bag and put it in a garbage can outside of your house. Even if you need to take it somewhere else, remove it from your home. Go to a gas station or somewhere with trash cans outside and dispose of it there.

If you would like to print out a certificate of this blessing, go to our website at *www.fathersblessing.info/resources.php* and print the "**Daughter's Blessing Certificate.**"

You can also watch a video of the Father's Blessing at *www.fathersblessing.info/daughters-blessing.php*

If you're a girl over the age of 14 and no one has ever told you that you're a woman, I want to do that for you now.

Passage into Womanhood

So many people have never heard, "You're a grown-up now; you're the age of an adult." Most girls have never heard anyone say, "Now you're a woman. You're no longer a child."

I believe a shift happens when a loving, caring parent tells you that you're now a woman and not a little girl anymore. There are many cultures that have ceremonies to mark the passage into adulthood. I want to share that moment with you right now.

If you're over the age of 14 (no matter how old you are), I, Papa Ray – as your spiritual father – declare that you're a woman, and you're no longer a girl. From this day forward, I bless you as a woman.

Always remember this day – today you were recognized as a woman. Write this down, sign it, and date it.

To help make this more significant, take a towel and lay it over your shoulders. Grasp the towel with your right hand and repeat the following:

"I was a girl. Now [take the towel and pull it off your shoulders] I'm a woman. I'm no longer a child. I think as a woman, and I act as a woman – because I *am* a woman. I'm loved and accepted as a woman. Everything I do is as a woman – because I'm no longer a child!"

Awesome! Now you know – no matter what age you are – that you truly are a woman! As your spiritual father, I bless you as a woman! You, my love, are an amazing woman!

Here's a sample of what you can write to mark your passage into womanhood.

"On this date, [today's date], I, [your name], am recognized by my spiritual father as a woman. I'm no longer a child. I'm an adult. I'm a woman."

"I, [your name], am a woman, and I'm powerful."

"I, [your name], am a woman, and I'm beautiful."

"I, [your name], am a woman, and I'm loved with pure love."

"I, [your name], am a woman, and I'm accepted."

Awesome! Now, you know – no matter what age you are – that you truly are a woman! As your spiritual father, I bless you as a woman! You, my love, are an amazing woman!

You can download and print this certificate by going to our website at *www.fathersblessing.info/resources.php* and printing out the "**Certificate of Womanhood**."

Welcome to the Family

As my daughter – welcome to my family of spiritual children! I'm so honored to receive you as part of my family. You're a worthy daughter, and you're worthy to be loved and blessed. You're worthy of reaching out and catching your dreams.

I challenge you to rise to a new level – no matter what you're doing or what you've done. I know you can be more and that you'll rise above whatever has held you down – because you're totally awesome!

I'm so excited because this is a new beginning – a new chapter in your life! You're at the threshold of your new life! It'll never be the same after this; things will change around you like never before. You'll start to see things and people differently; you'll see life in a whole new way. Today is the first day of the rest of your new life! I'm so proud of you for overcoming the obstacles you've faced. You'll never be the same again. You'll become better and better with each passing day. You'll learn to believe in yourself!

Please remember this: "One day at a time; one step at a time." You're on a journey. It takes time to complete each step. Don't rush to the next level; allow it to play out, or you'll have to repeat it again.

The Ultimate Blessing

I believe the earthly father's blessing is critically important. However, there's a blessing that's so much greater! No matter how right or wrong our earthly father is, your Father in Heaven loves you even more. He loves you with an endless love – a perfect love!

- He isn't a part-time or absent Father.

- He's never too busy or too tired to sit and listen.

- He's never on vacation or off the clock.

- He never turns His phone off.

He loves you so much that He gave His Son, Jesus Christ, to suffer and die upon the cross. He paid the price for your sins so you can be free from them. You don't have to be perfect; you don't have to raise yourself to a certain standard before

He accepts you as one of His children. He loves you and wants you just as you are. That's right – just as you are.

The greatest part is that it's easy to receive His blessings – He simply wants to give them to you. He isn't a harsh, angry old man in the sky – waiting for you to mess up so He can throw lightning bolts at you. Our Heavenly Father is a kind, gentle, and loving Father who wants to give you the greatest gift – the ultimate blessing: Eternal life. Because He loves you so much, He wants you to be with Him in Heaven – forever. Our Father God in Heaven tells us in His love letter that He gave His Son so that whoever (that's you!) believes in Him won't perish – but will have eternal life. That's from John 3:16 in the Bible.

Stop and Reflect

- Do you want to feel peace and love in your heart?

- Do you want to know – with assurance – that you're loved with an everlasting love?

- Would you like to invite Jesus Christ into your heart as your Lord and Savior – giving you eternal life and abundance?

Here's an easy-to-follow, step-by-step way to welcome Jesus Christ to fill your heart with His peace and love. It's called the "Romans Road" because these verses are all from the book of Romans.

The Romans Road of Salvation, Key Scriptures

1. Everyone needs salvation because we've all sinned.

Romans 3:10–12, 23: "No one is righteous – not even one. No one is truly wise; no one is seeking God. All have turned away; all have become useless. No one does good, not a single one." "For everyone has sinned; we all fall short of God's glorious standard."

2. The price (or consequence) of sin is death.

Romans 6:23: "For the wages of sin is death, but the free gift of God is eternal life through Christ Jesus, our Lord."

3. Jesus Christ died for our sins. He paid the price for our death so our spirit doesn't have to die.

Romans 5:8: "But God showed his great love for us by sending Christ to die for us while we were still sinners."

4. We receive salvation and eternal life through faith in Jesus Christ.

134

Romans 10:9–10, 13: "If you confess with your mouth that Jesus is Lord and believe in your heart that God raised him from the dead, you will be saved. For it is by believing in your heart that you are made right with God and it is by confessing with your mouth that you are saved, for everyone who calls on the name of the Lord will be saved."

5. Salvation through Jesus Christ brings us into a relationship of peace with God.

Romans 5:1: "Therefore, since we have been made right in God's sight by faith, we have peace with God because of what Jesus Christ our Lord has done for us."

Romans 8:1: "So now there is no condemnation for those who belong to Christ Jesus."

Romans 8:38–39: "And I am convinced that nothing can ever separate us from God's love. Neither death nor life, neither angels nor demons, neither our fears for today nor our worries about tomorrow, not even the powers of hell can separate us from God's love. No power in the sky above or in the earth below indeed, nothing in all creation will ever be able to separate us from the love of God that is revealed in Christ Jesus our Lord."

All verses are from the New Living Translation Bible.

Responding to the Romans Road

If you believe what you read in these verses, respond by receiving God's free gift of salvation today. Here's how to take a personal journey down the Romans Road:

1. Admit you're a sinner.
2. Understand that as a sinner, you deserve death.
3. Believe that Jesus Christ died upon the cross to save you from sin and death.
4. Repent by turning from your old life of sin to a new life in Christ.
5. Receive – through faith in Jesus Christ – His free gift of salvation.

Here's a sample prayer:

> "Dear Father God in Heaven, I come to You in the name of Jesus Christ. I acknowledge to You that I'm a sinner, and I'm sorry for my sins and the life I've lived; I need Your forgiveness."

> "I believe Your only begotten Son, Jesus Christ, shed His precious blood upon the cross at Calvary and died for my sins. I'm willing to turn from my sin right now."

"You said in Your Holy Word, (Romans 10:9) that if I confess with my mouth that Jesus is Lord and believe in my heart that You raised Him from the dead, I will be saved."

If you can, it's important to speak this part aloud.

"I confess that I want you, Jesus Christ, to be the Lord of my soul. With all my heart, I believe God raised You from the dead, Jesus. In this very moment, I accept You, Jesus Christ, as my personal Savior. According to Your Word, I'm saved."

"I thank You, Jesus, for Your unlimited grace – which has saved me from my sins. I thank You, Jesus, that Your grace never leads to bondage – but always leads to repentance. Therefore, Lord Jesus, help me to choose wisely so my life will bring glory and honor to You alone and not to myself."

"Thank you, Jesus, for dying for me and giving me eternal life. Amen."

If you would like to print out and sign a copy of this prayer, please go to our website at *www.fathersblessing.info/resources.php* and print out the "**Salvation Prayer**."

Welcome to the family of believers – the spiritual family of Jesus Christ! Your life will never be the same. Your newfound faith is a learning process; this isn't a one-time cure-all for every problem. As a believer, your next steps are to:

- Read your Bible daily to be filled with the Word of God – the truth – so you won't be deceived. Find a good, Bible-believing church that isn't afraid to speak the truth.

- Be baptized with water.

- Make all efforts to live in peace with everyone.

- Live well, love strong, and be kind to all people.

The Christian life is a learning experience. Like all the rest of us, you have a lifetime of learning ahead of you. It's a journey and will only be what you make it. You'll get out of it what you put into it. If you only approach this half-heartedly, don't expect to have a blessed life of peace. Allowing Jesus Christ to be Lord of your life is to go "all in" or not at all. Living a real Christian life isn't something you only do when you want to and jump out of when it isn't fun. This life could be the hardest thing you ever do. However, the rewards are out of this world!

There's nothing that could compare to the real peace and joy that comes when you totally and completely turn your life over to Jesus Christ!

Once again, welcome to the family!

In Conclusion

First of all, I'm so glad you've taken the time to read this book and to receive the Father's Blessing! You now know you're blessed and loved as a daughter! If you took this blessing to heart – no matter where you've been or what you've done – you're a new person!

Life won't be perfect now that you have this blessing. You are, however, stronger, and you'll be able to stand against the struggles of the world because you know you're loved and wanted. You're a woman, and you're powerful! Keep pressing on, and don't let life pass you by. If you want more, you must keep pressing on in order to get it. Life will only return what you give. Just like putting money into a savings account with a high return, the more you put in, the more you'll get back.

Here are a few things I highly recommend in order to help you get a higher return on your time.

Accountability

The number-one priority for anyone – at any level in life – is to have an accountability group with like-minded people of the same gender. As much as you need to be accountable to your spouse – if you're married – you still need to be in an accountability group of people of the same gender and with the same core values. If you want to see any progress, this is important – life has a way of flying past before you know what happened. Days and years can go by while you're still in the same place!

This should be a closed group of four to eight people that meet at least once a month. In this group, people should be encouraged to share anything. It should be a group of peers who want to support one another. There should be no fees to join. Once the group is established, everyone must agree before anyone else can join the group.

A Coach or Mentor

The next significant step is to hire a coach or mentor. If you want to get your life on the fast track to improvement, you need a coach who isn't afraid to hold your feet to the fire. Whatever you do, never use a friend who's afraid to tell you that you're crazy. Your coach should be willing to stop you in the middle of a sentence and tell you never to say it again.

When you break it down, you're paying someone to tell you the truth. Do you want to spend money for someone to listen to you talk about something that may never happen – just so you have a chance to speak? Or do you want to get on with life and build your legacy? If you want to make it happen, you'll need a coach or mentor who's willing to speak the harsh truth – no matter how much it hurts.

Prayer and Meditation

Prayer and meditation should be the number-one priorities in your daily life – to keep you rooted and grounded. It's easy for life to get out of control before you know it. Prayer and meditation will help bring your life back to the center and eliminate the noise. If you never stop to think about what you're thinking, you'll never weed out the incorrect information that builds up in your mind.

Every day, pray for guidance and wisdom from the Lord, then meditate upon the truth you hear. You'll learn to hold on to what you know is true, and the lies will fall away.

Once again, thank you for reading this book. If you've been blessed, please share this with anyone you feel would benefit from receiving this blessing as well.

Stay in Touch

If you would like to stay in touch and get my latest updates, please visit our website, and sign up for our email list. We'll keep you informed of any seminars, conferences, new books, or any other resources we make available. We're always writing new material and would love to share it with you!

You can contact us or sign up for the newsletter at
www.fathersblessing.info/contact.php

Invite Papa Ray to Speak

Please contact us to have Papa Ray speak at your event. Ray is an international speaker and has spoken many times on the importance of fathers in the home. Papa Ray's heart's desire is to touch the broken hearts of the people around the world and to leave God's fingerprints upon them. Contact us at:

www.fathersblessing.info/invite.php

Sponsor a Father's Blessing Event

Ray has traveled near and far to share the Father's Blessing. Some of the best times have been in a group setting. Please contact us if you would like your church or group to sponsor a Father's Blessing event at *www.fathersblessing.info/invite.php*

Be sure to follow me on Facebook at

www.facebook.com/fathersblessing

Coaching and Training

As a personal transformation coach, Ray has been able to help a lot of people find their purpose and passion in life. He's had a very high success rate in helping to restore marriages and families.

If you would like to get more information on any of the coaching programs – from one-to-one personal coaching to the money-back-guaranteed intense three-day in-home marriage immersion, please visit our website at www.ILAPnow.com.

Appendix

- 63% of youth suicides are from fatherless homes. (Source: U.S. D.H.H.S., Bureau of the Census)

- 90% of all homeless and runaway children are from fatherless homes. (The National Center for Fathering)

- 85% of all children that exhibit behavioral disorders come from fatherless homes. (Source: Center for Disease Control)

- 80% of rapists motivated by displaced anger come from fatherless homes. (Source: Criminal Justice & Behavior, Vol 14, p. 403-26, 1978)

- 71% of all high school dropouts come from fatherless homes. (Source: National Principals Association Report on the State of High Schools)

- 75% of all adolescent patients in chemical abuse centers come from fatherless homes. (Source: Rainbows for all God's Children)

- 70% of juveniles in state-operated institutions come from fatherless homes. (Source: U.S. Dept. of Justice, Special Report, Sept. 1988)

- 85% of all youths sitting in prisons grew up in a fatherless home. (Source: Fulton County Georgia jail populations, Texas Dept. of Corrections, 1992)

Because only a portion of each age group grew up in a fatherless home, these statistics translate to mean that children from fatherless homes are:

- 32 times more likely to run away.

- 20 times more likely to have behavioral disorders.

- 14 times more likely to commit rape.

- 9 times more likely to drop out of high school.

- 20 times more likely to end up in prison.

References

1. Taylor, R., & Taylor, G. (2008). *Love Hunger – The Unseen Force.*

2. Frost, T., & Frost, J. (2006). *Spiritual Slavery to Spiritual Sonship.* Destiny Image Publishers.

3. Peck, S. M. (2003). *The Road Less Traveled.* Touchstone.

4. Shelton, T., & Aronica, L. (2021). *The Greatest You: Face Reality, Release Negativity, and Live Your Purpose.* Thomas Nelson.

Researchers on Thoughts in Relation to Cellular Functions

Dr. Joe Dispenza

Dr. Bruce Lipton

Andrew Huberman, Ph.D. – Professor of Neuroscience & Lab Director at Stanford

Made in the USA
Middletown, DE
09 October 2023

40341901R00089